Reverie Illustrations

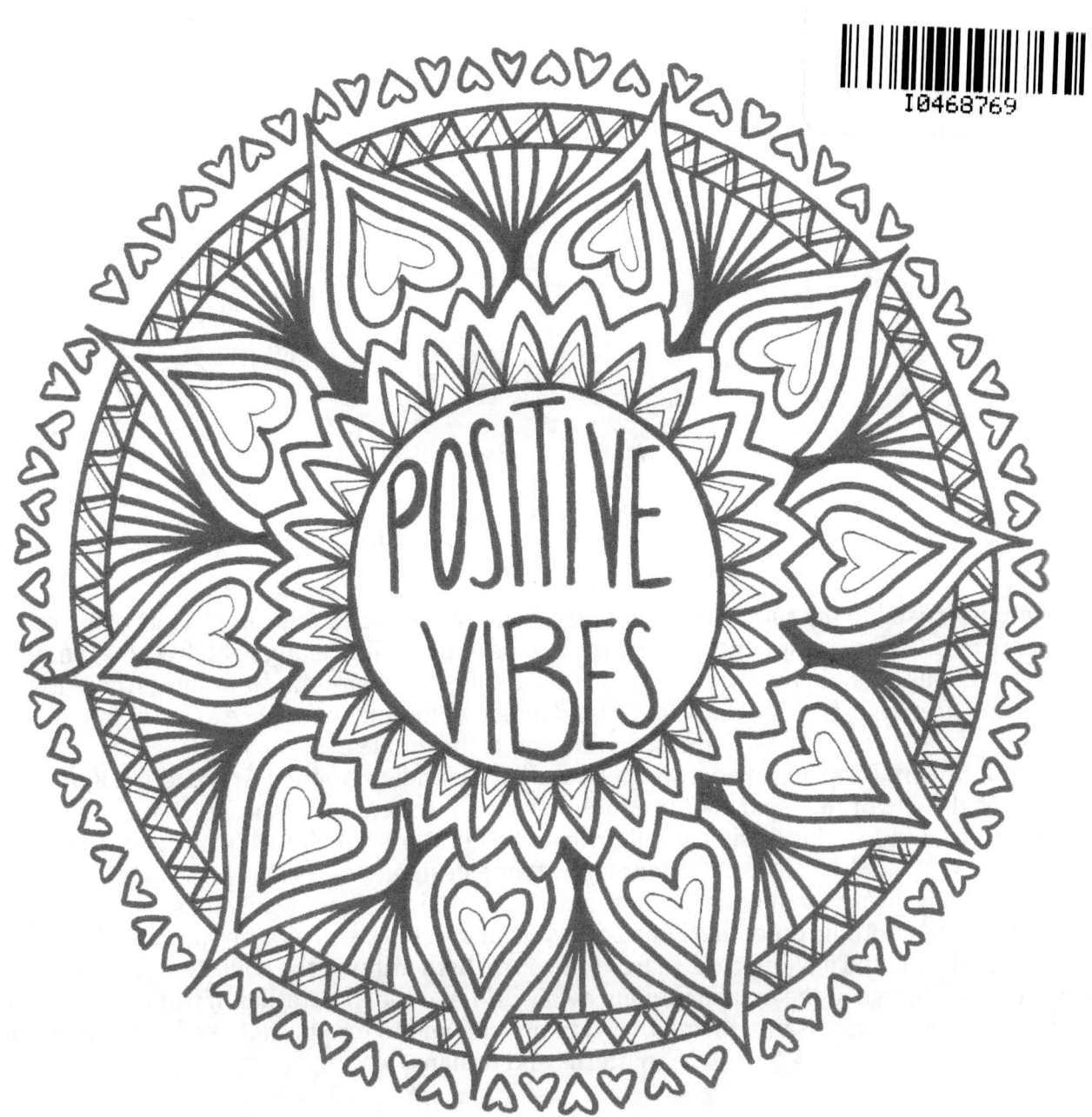

POSITIVE VIBES

Adult Coloring Book
30 hand drawn, hippie inspired designs

By Amber Scott

Reverie (def.)

/ˈrɛv(ə)ri/
A state of being pleasantly lost in thought, a state of dreamy meditation, a daydream.
Ex. "A knock on the door broke her reverie".
Synonyms: daydream, trance, fantasy, vision, hallucination, musing, etc.

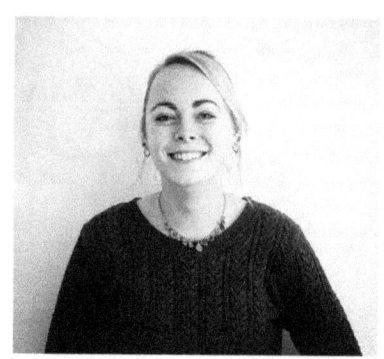

Autobiography

Born in Dublin, raised in the rural French countryside, my childhood was never short of adventures. The first ten years of my life were spent exploring rock pools and running along wild, freezing, empty beaches. The second part was spent in the lush countryside of the Poitou Charentes in France, where I was covered in muck more often than not. My days were spent looking after an abundance of farm animals, climbing trees, fishing and riding horses.

At the age of fifteen, I was accepted into a school where I studied Applied Arts and Design for the next three years. At the age of 18, I said goodbye to France and pursued my studies in Dun Laoghaire, Ireland. There, I specialized in Interior Design and Furniture Restoration, which fuelled my creativity and passion for art, craft and design.

As much as my days were spent outside, those rainy days and those quiet evenings were always set aside for coloring. There's nothing quite like lying sprawled on the floor with a rainbow of markers, pencils and crayons around you, and a blank page in front of you. Whether it was the collective group coloring with my two younger siblings or the escape into my own world and the illustration in front of me, coloring has always allowed me to express myself creatively; to unwind and to lose myself in a kaleidoscope of colors, patterns and designs.

ISBN-13: 978-1530757190
ISBN-10: 1530757193

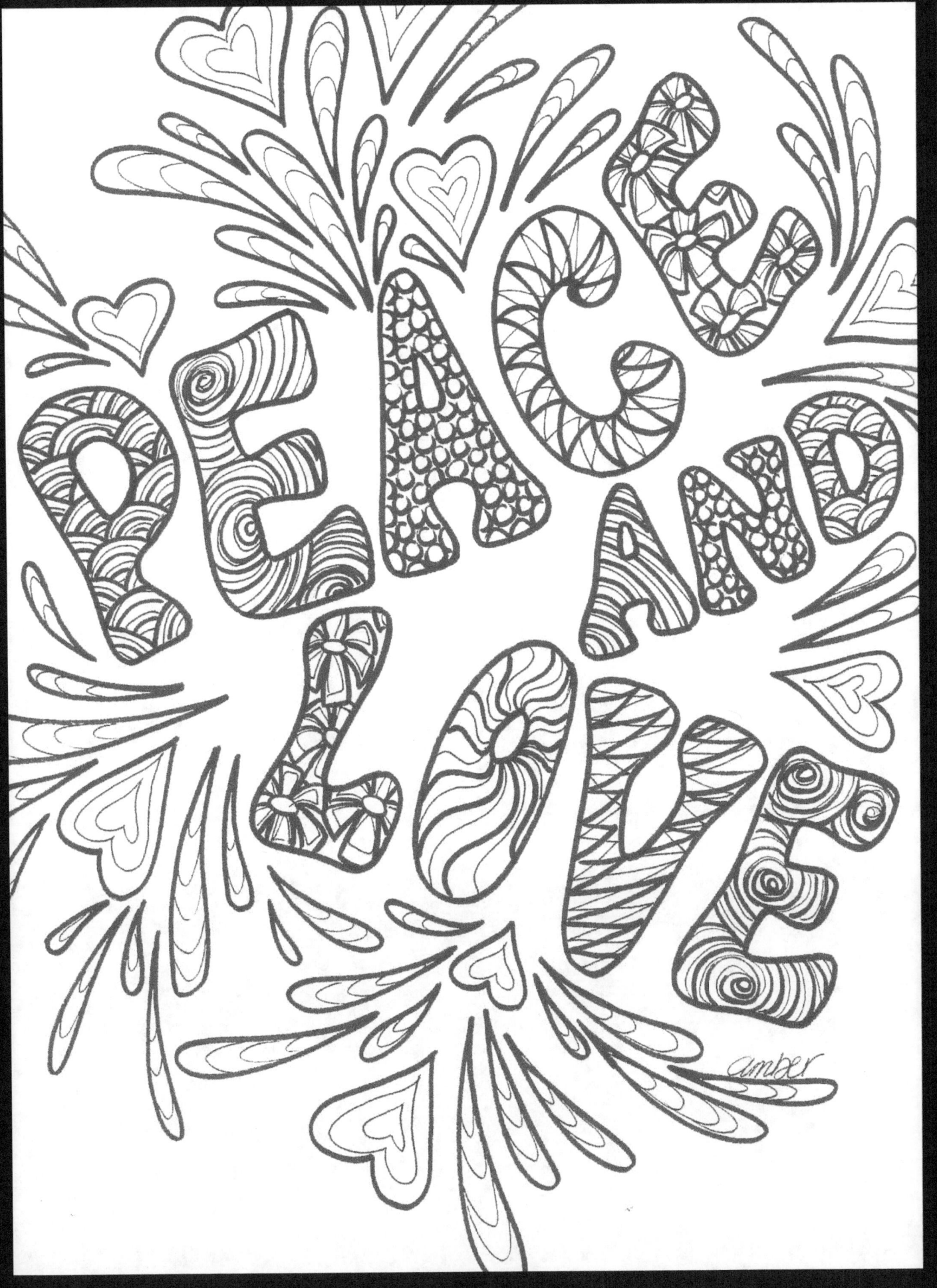

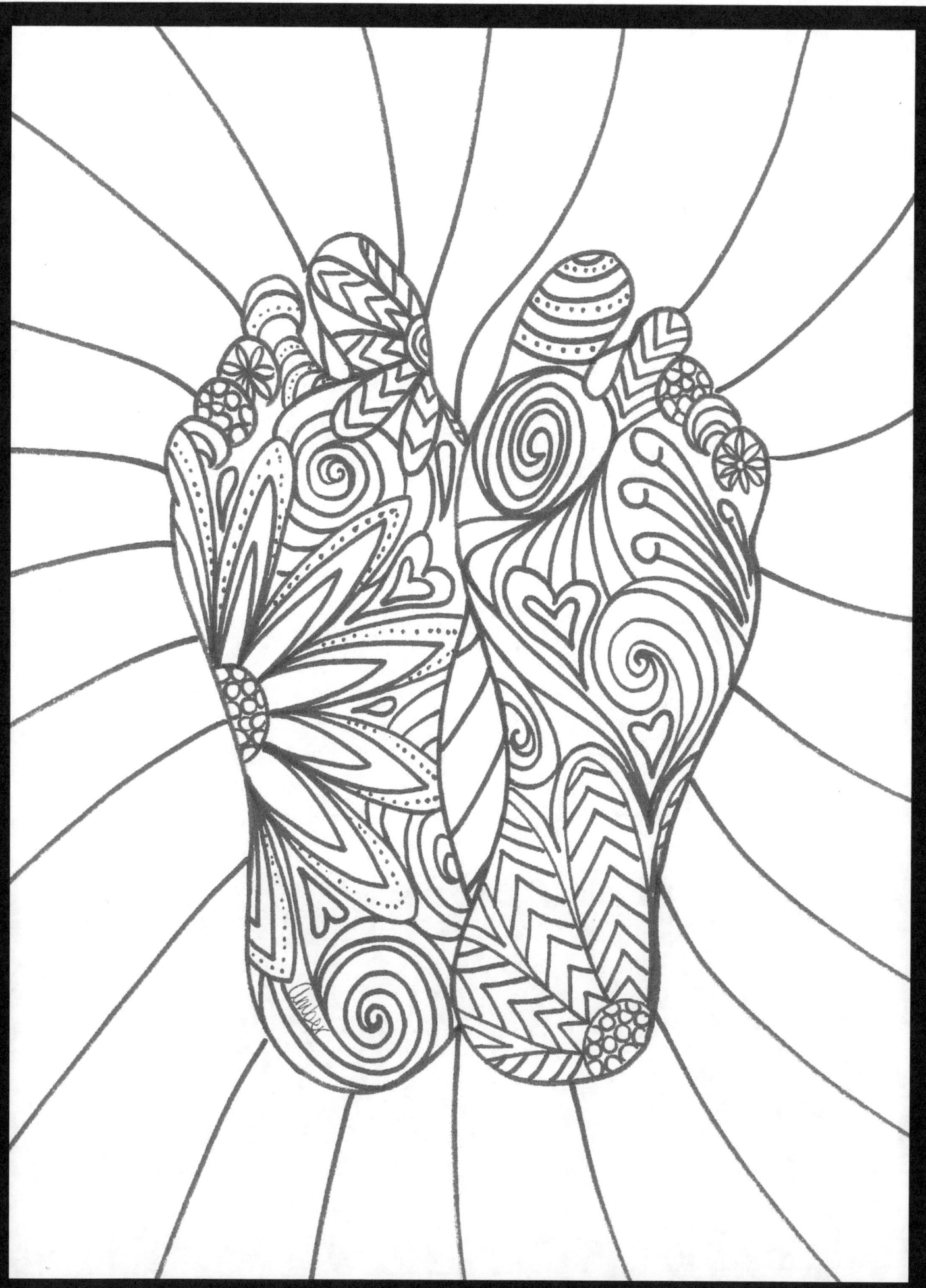

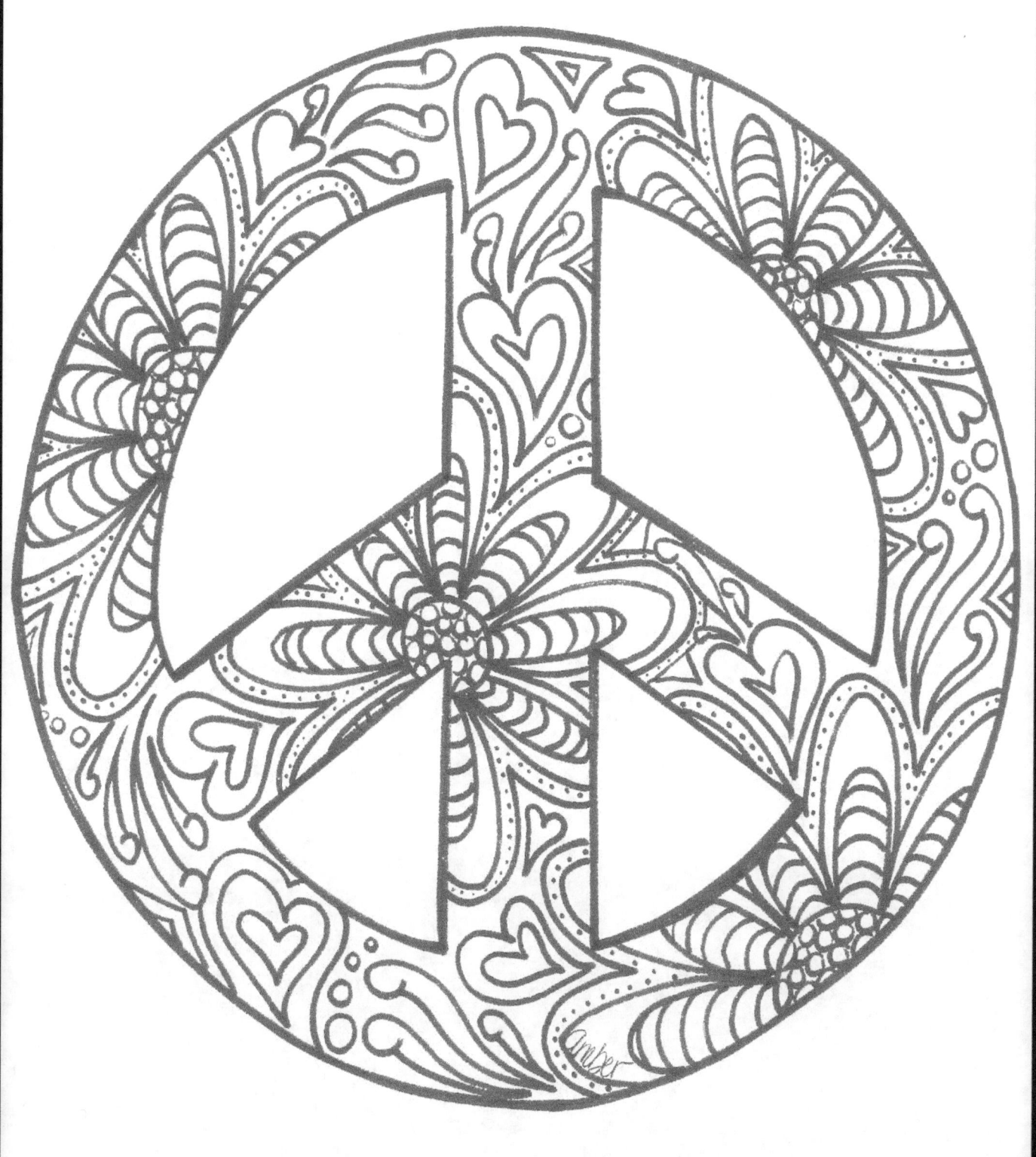

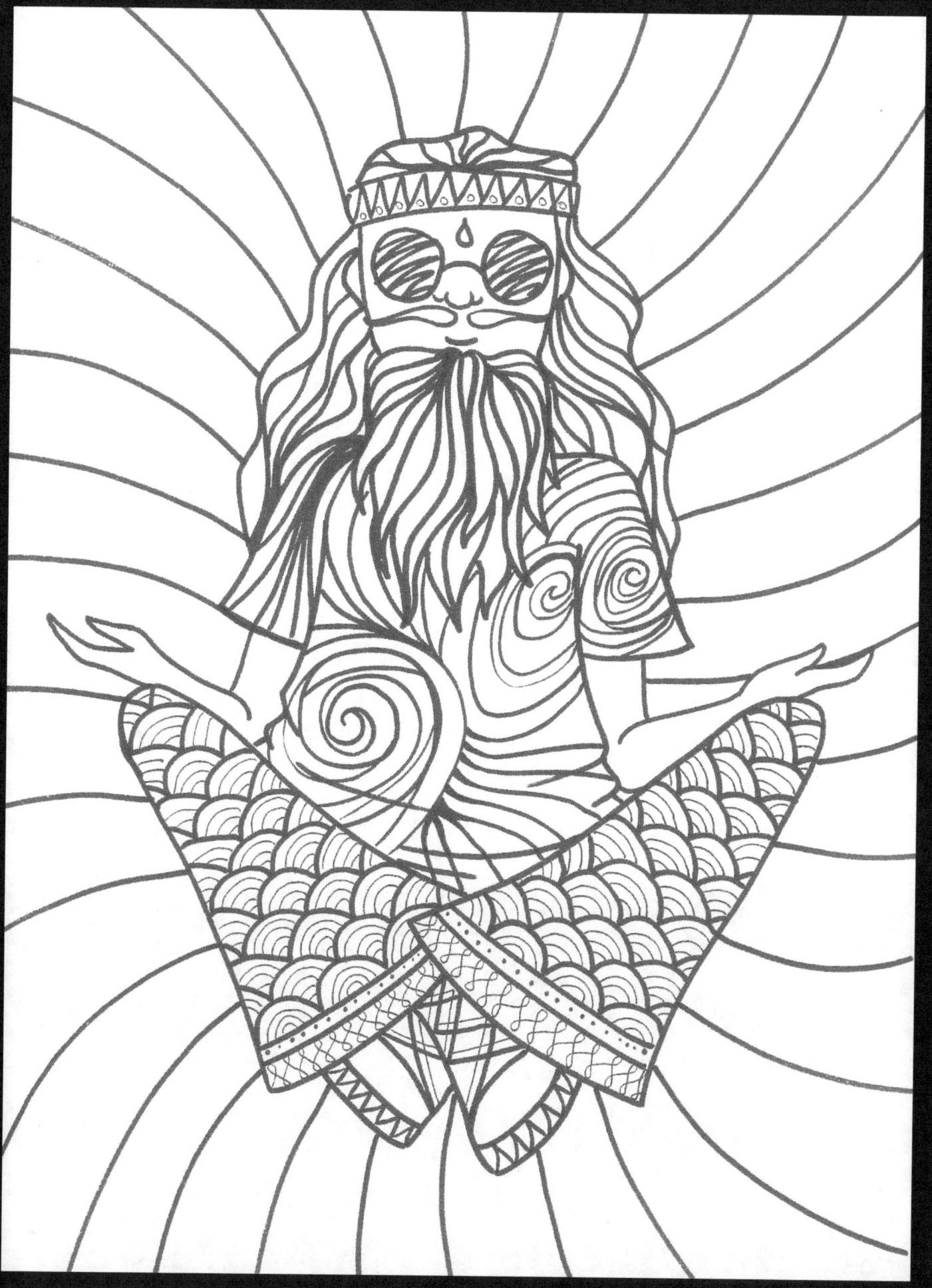

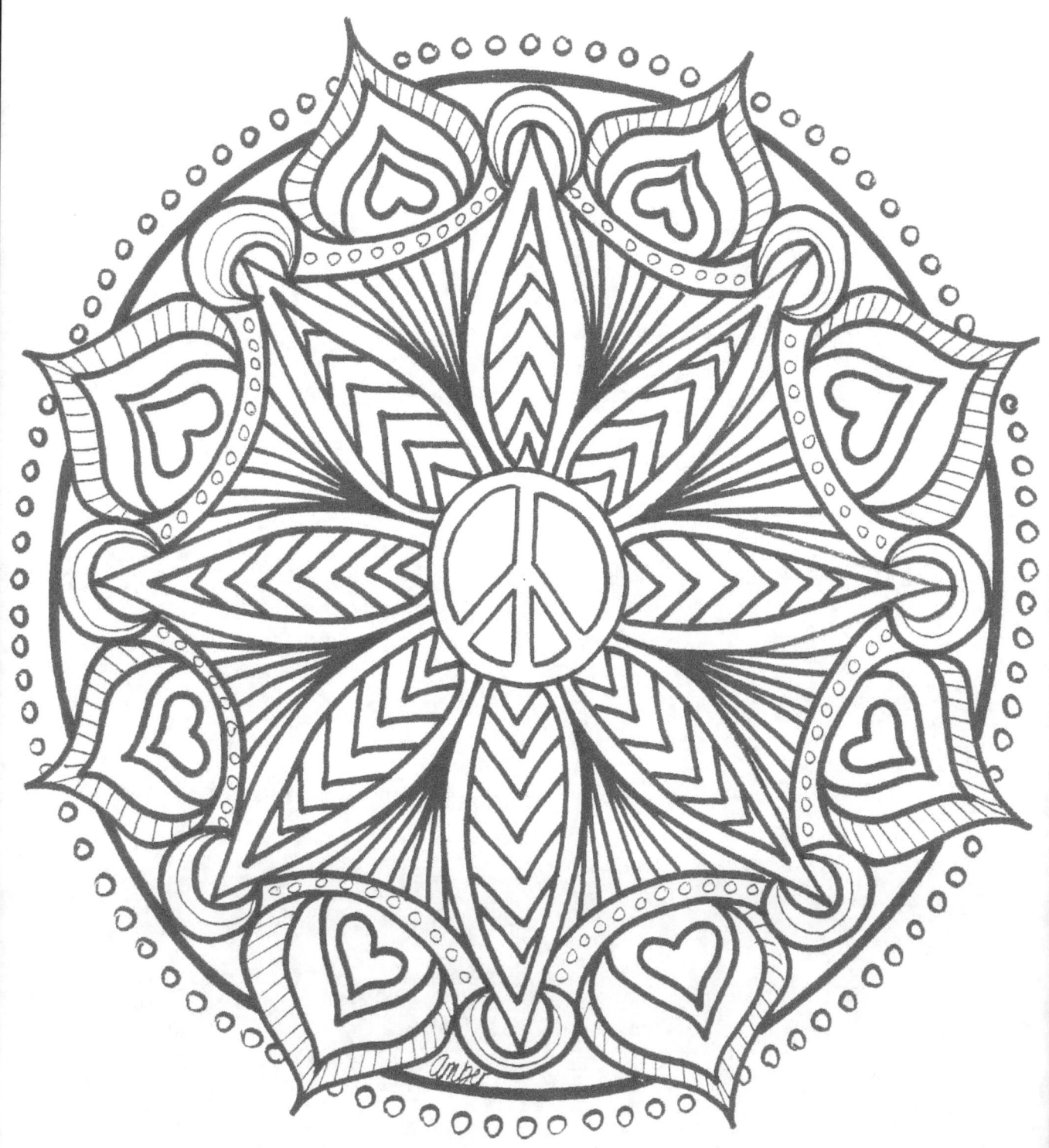

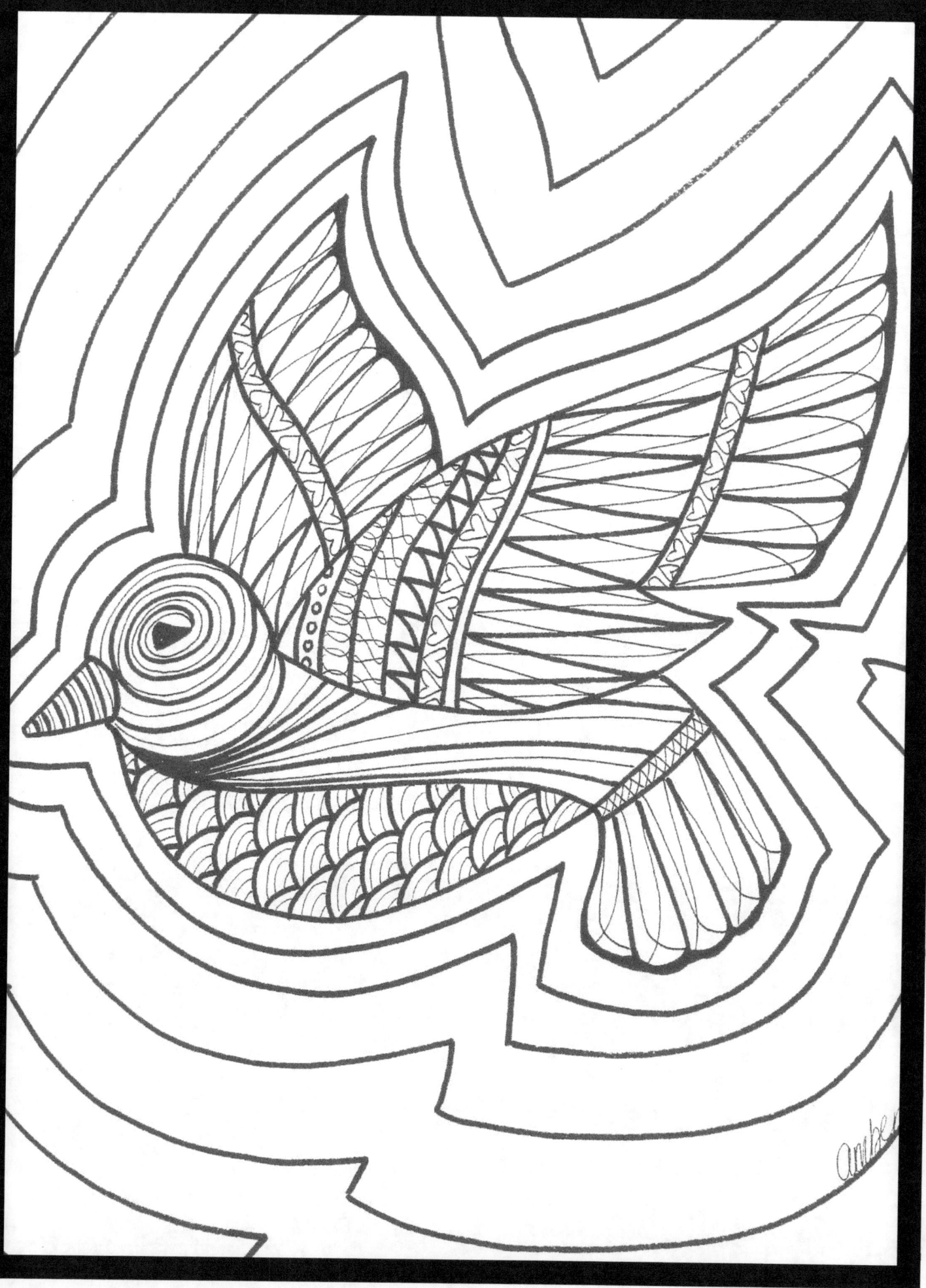

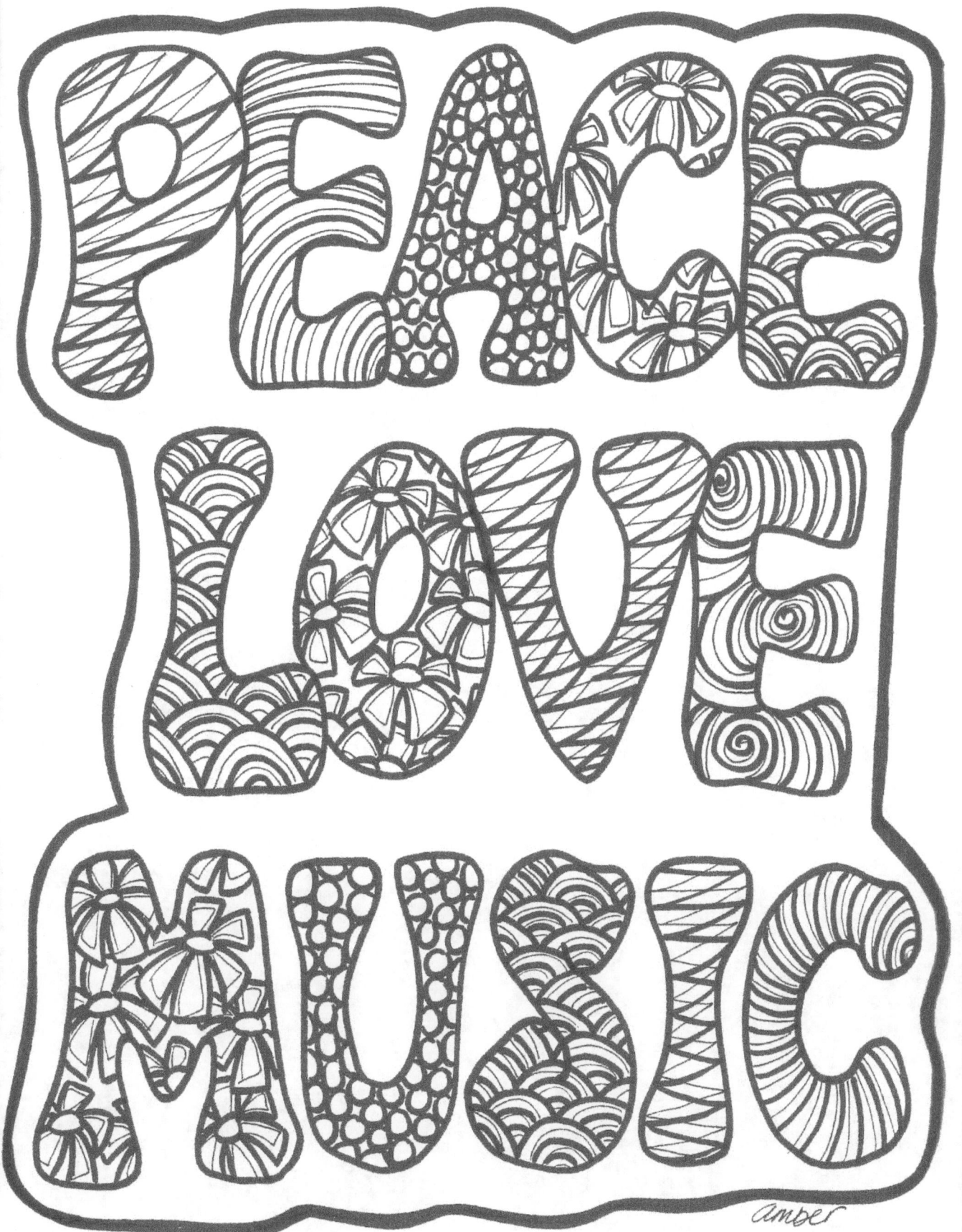

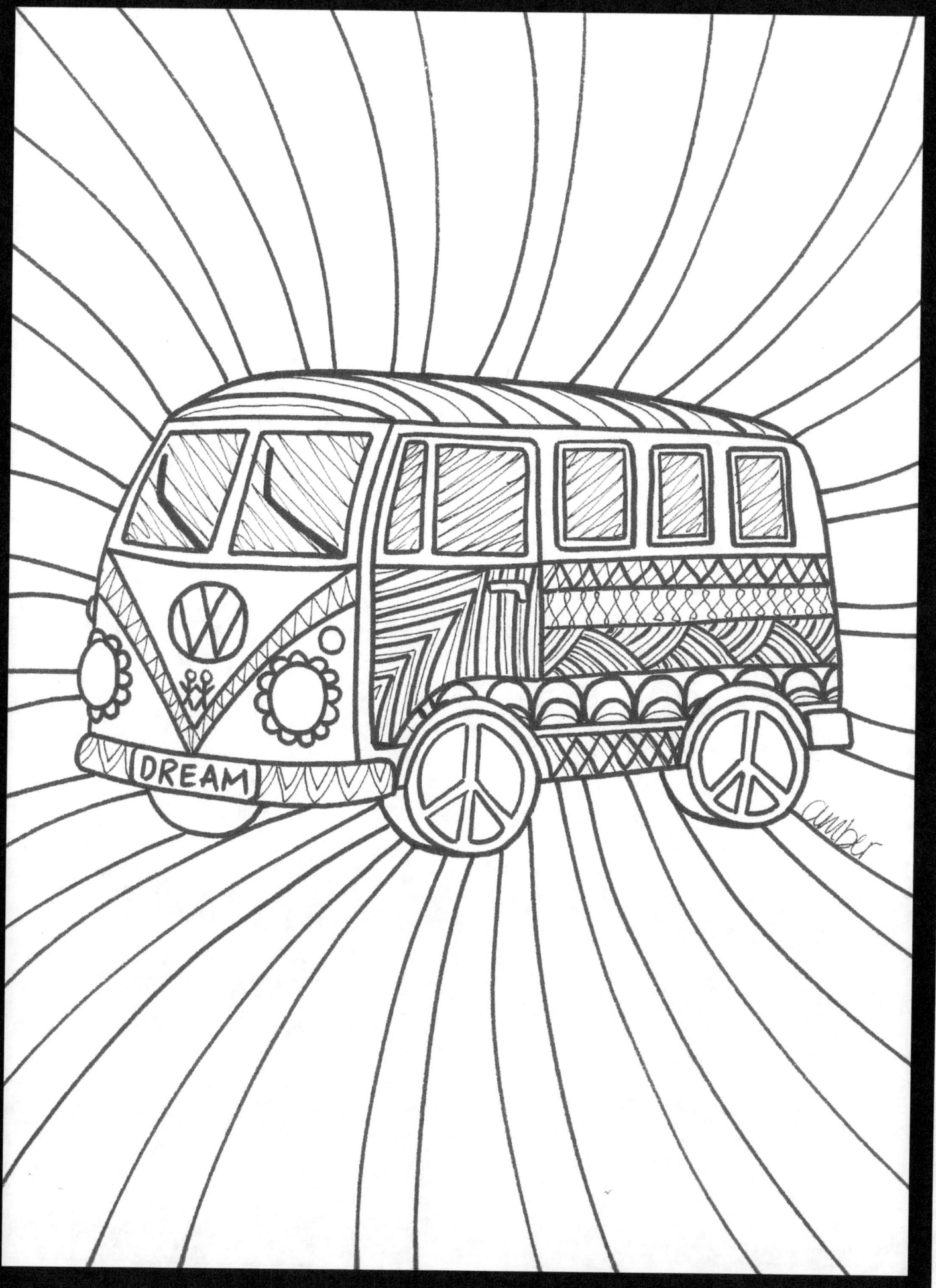

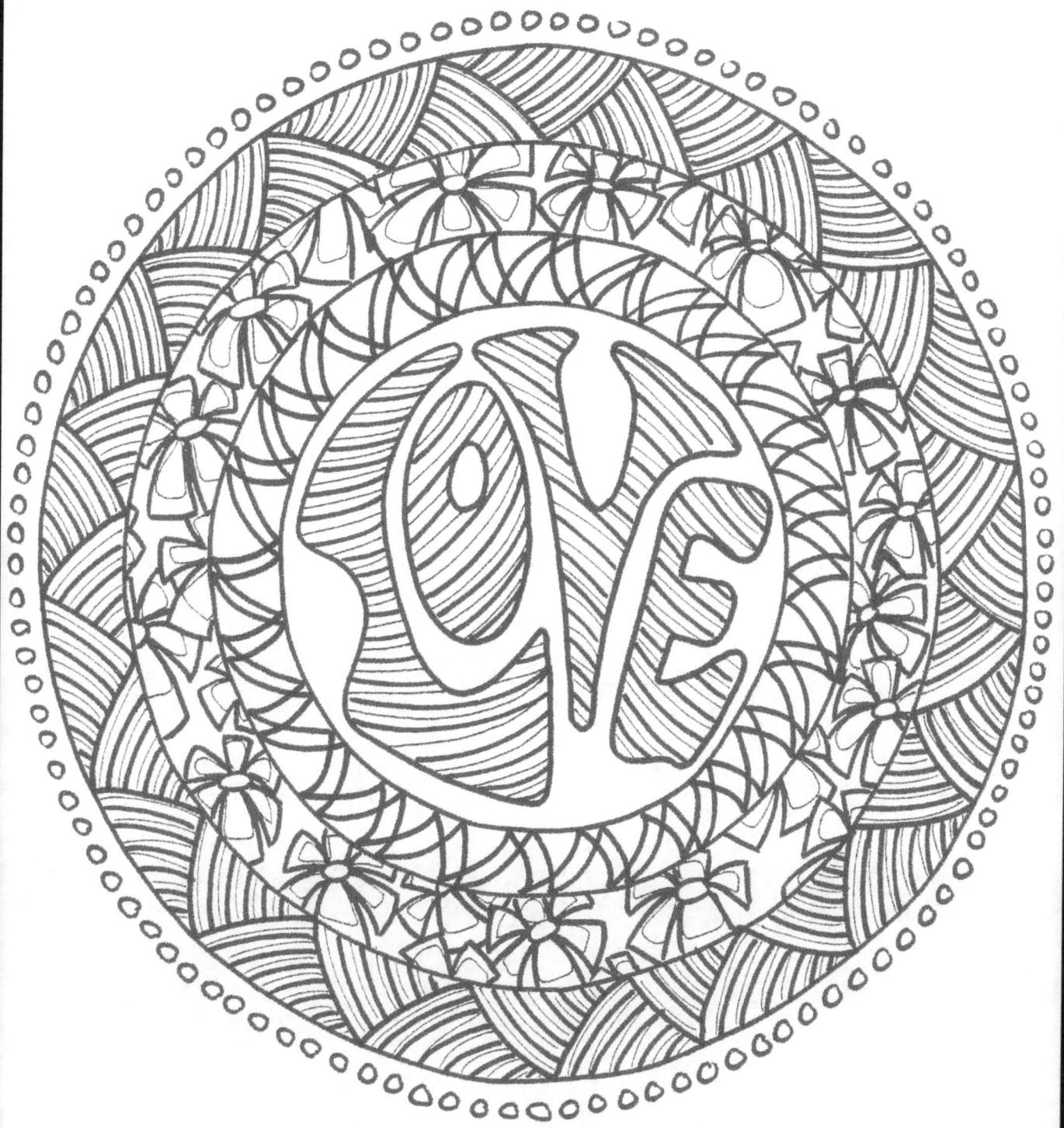

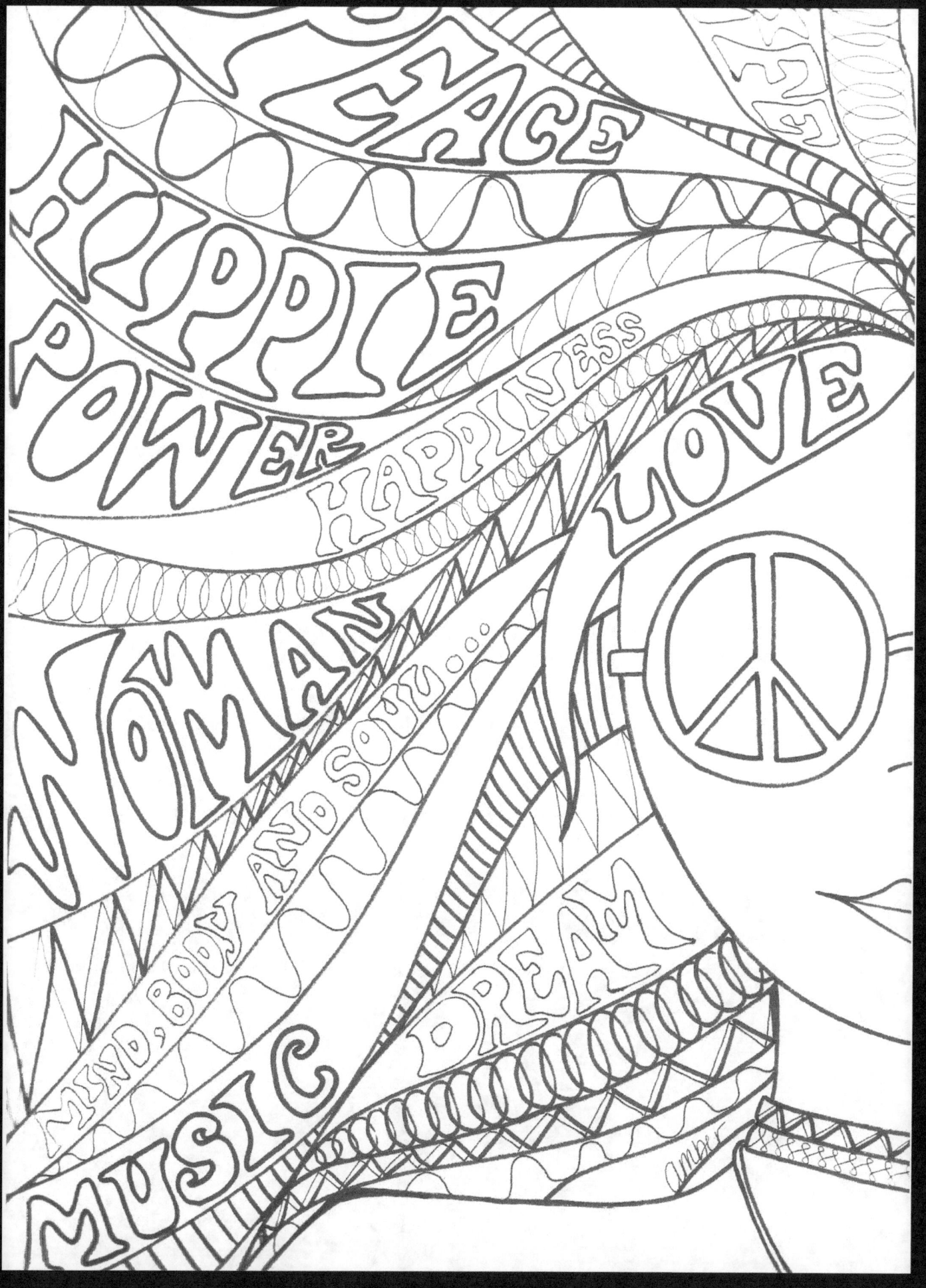

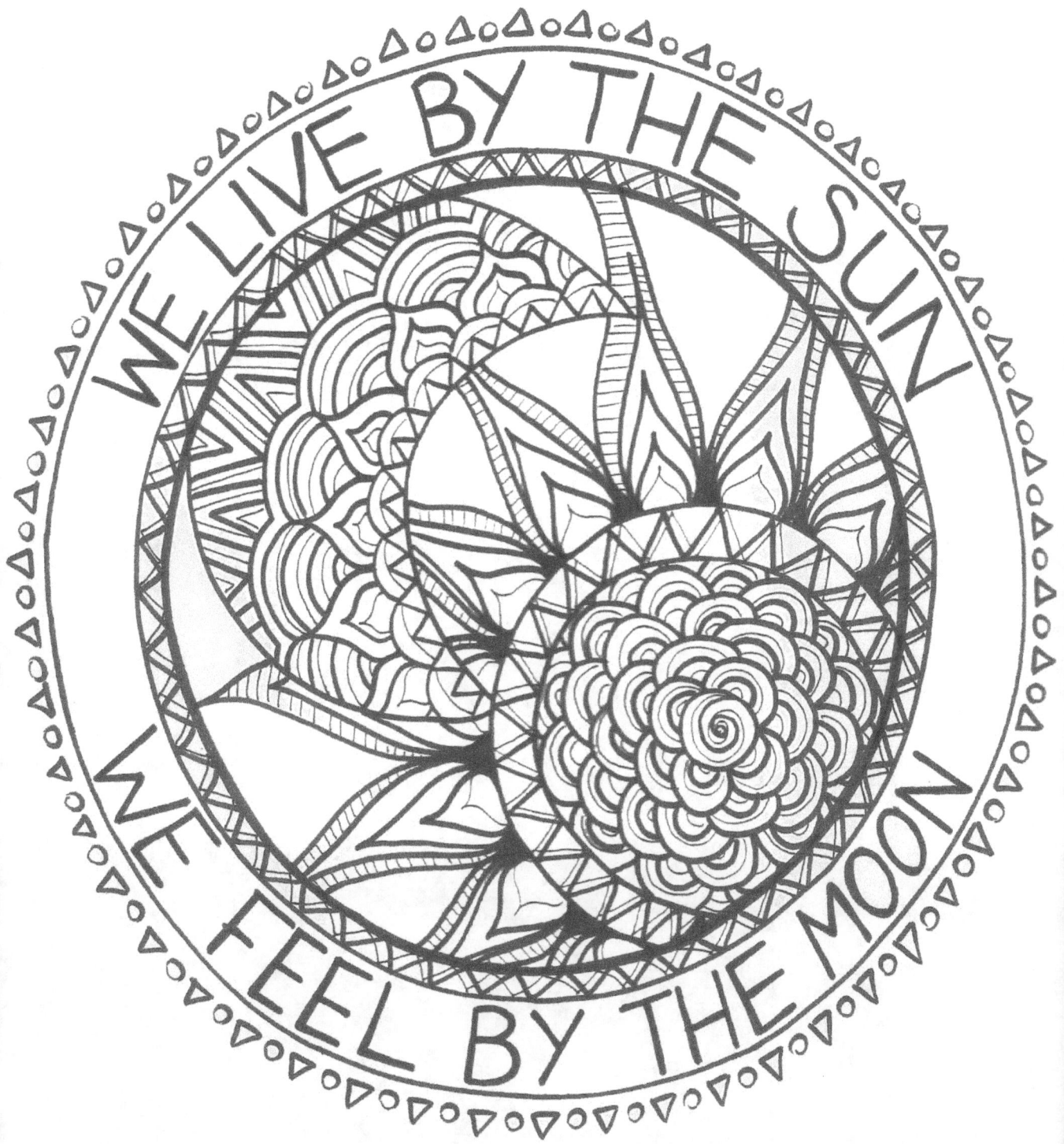

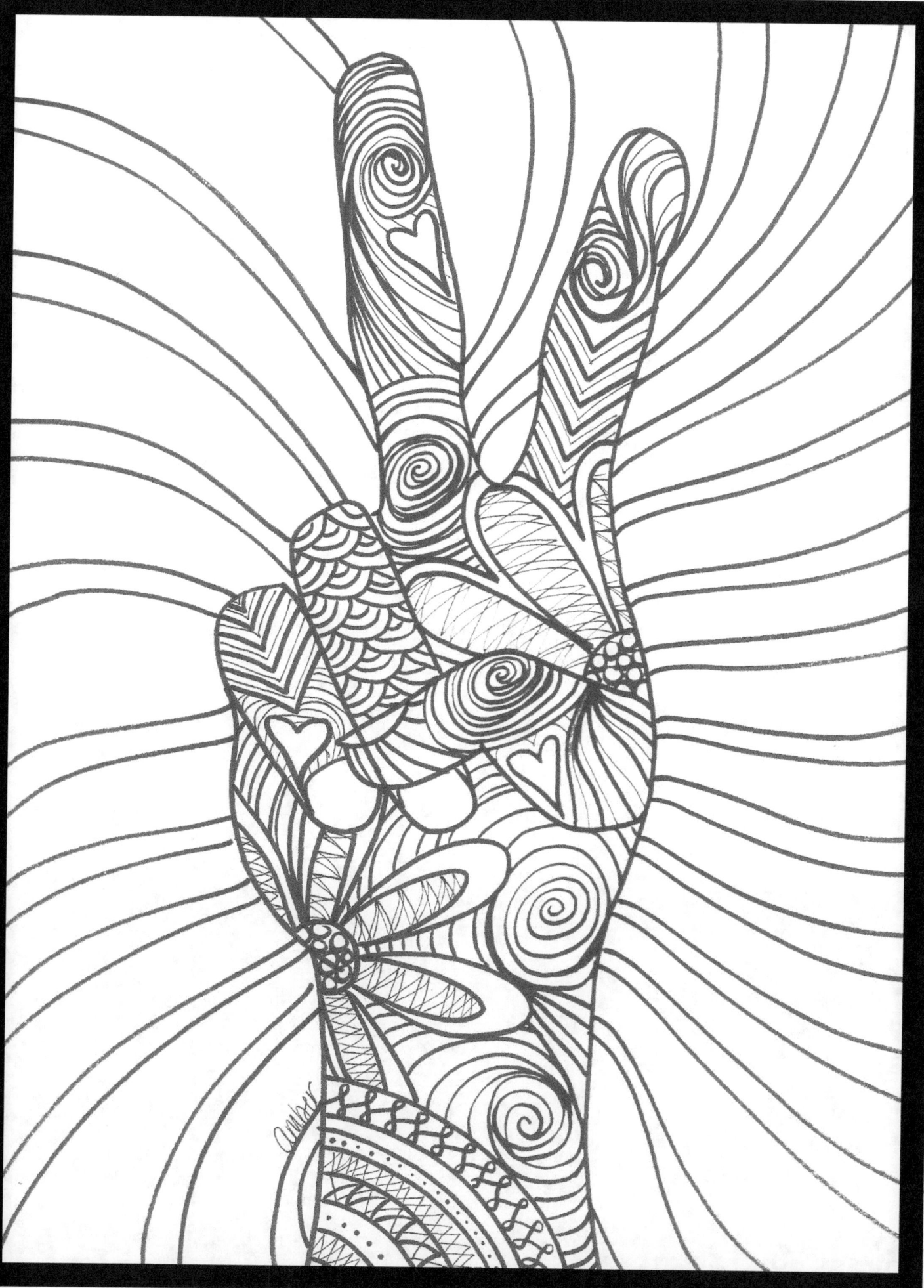

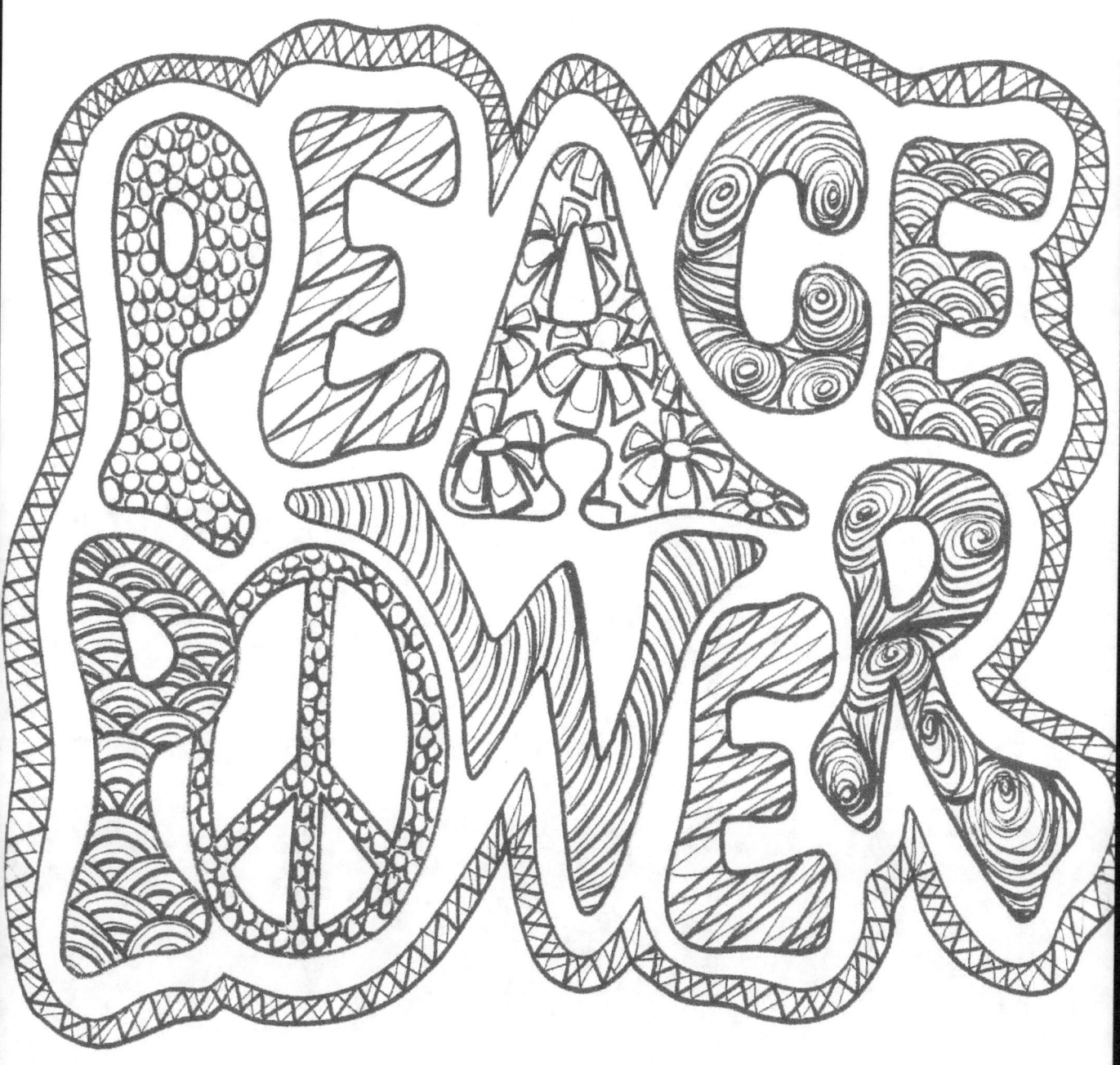

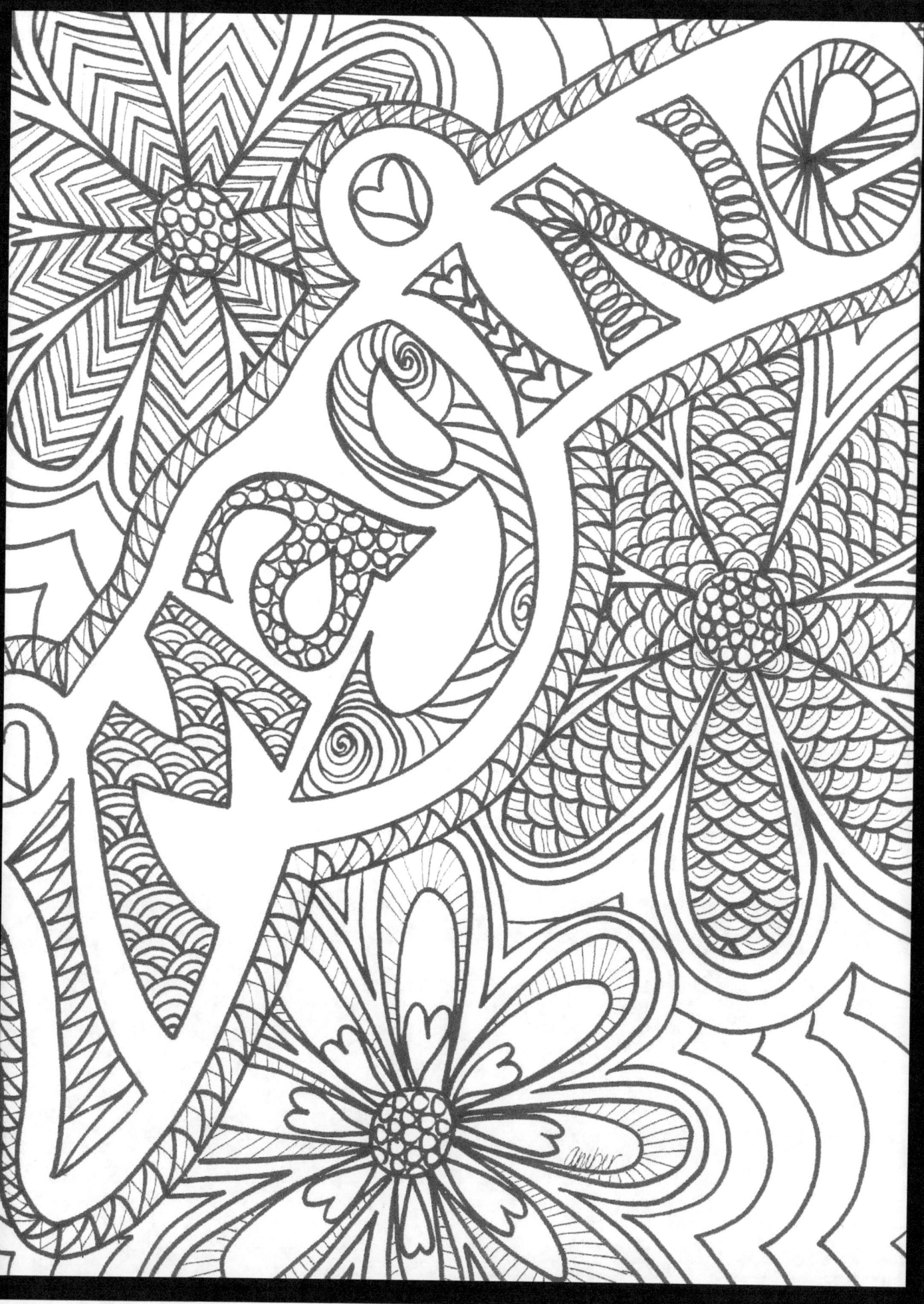

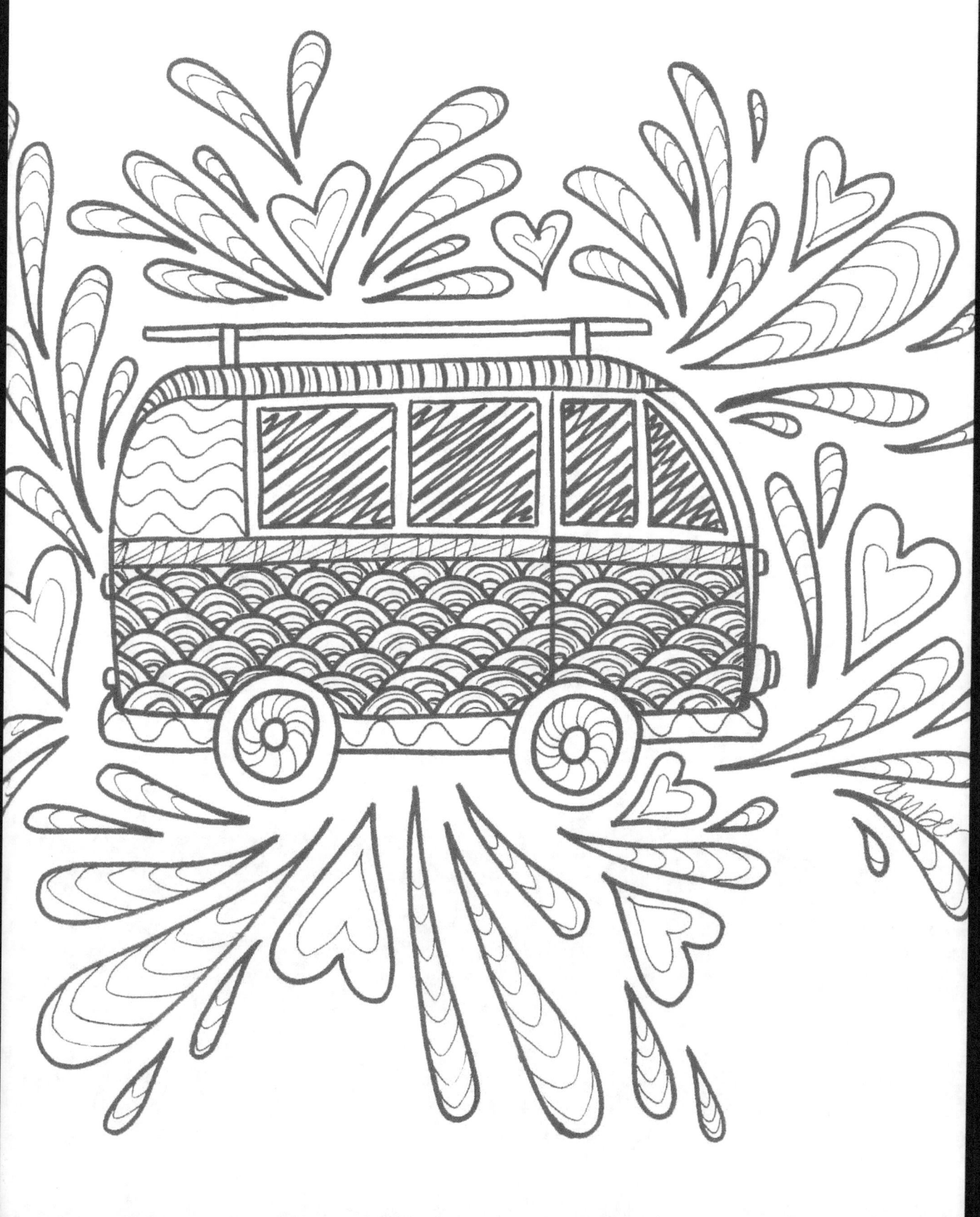

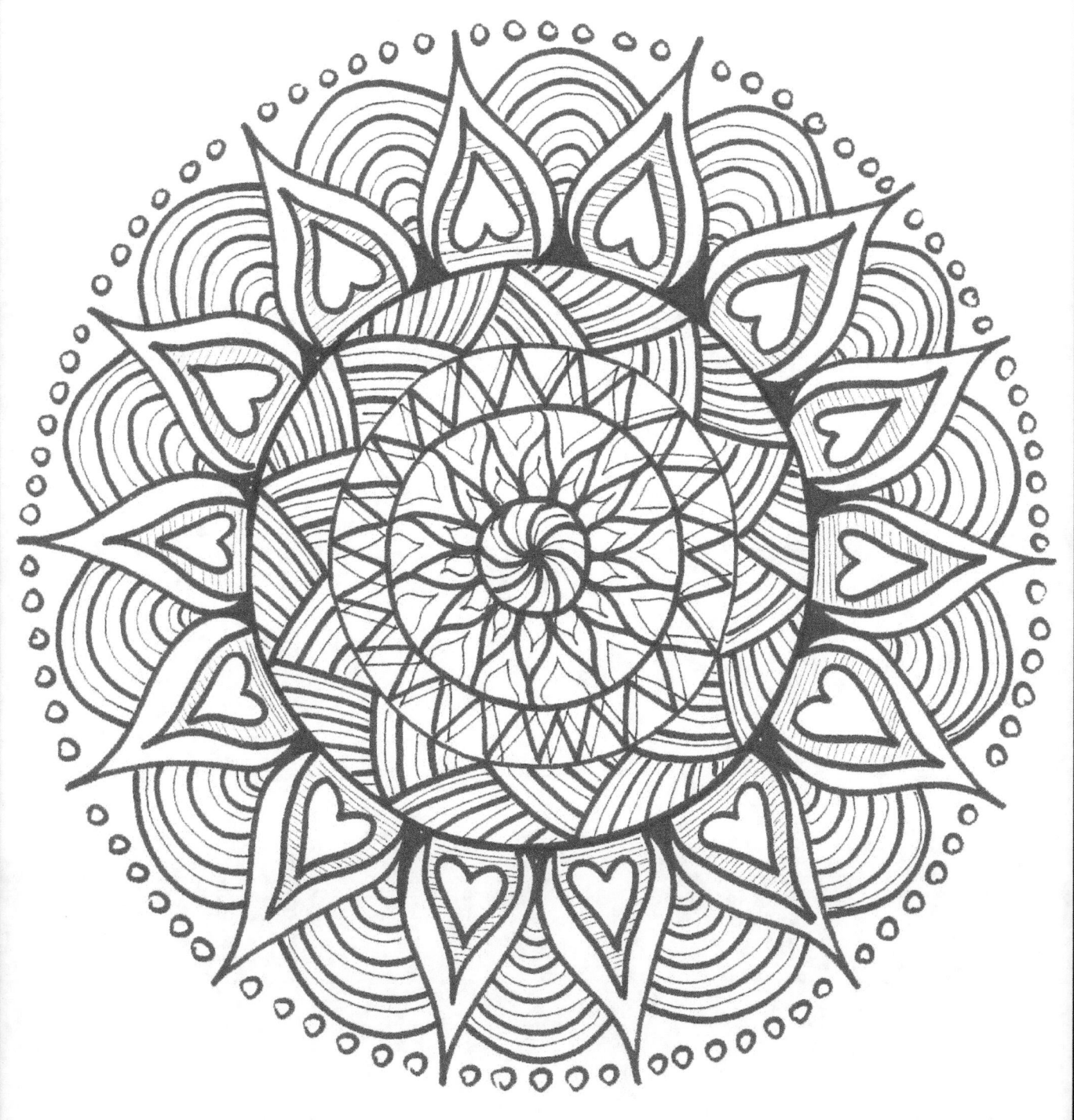

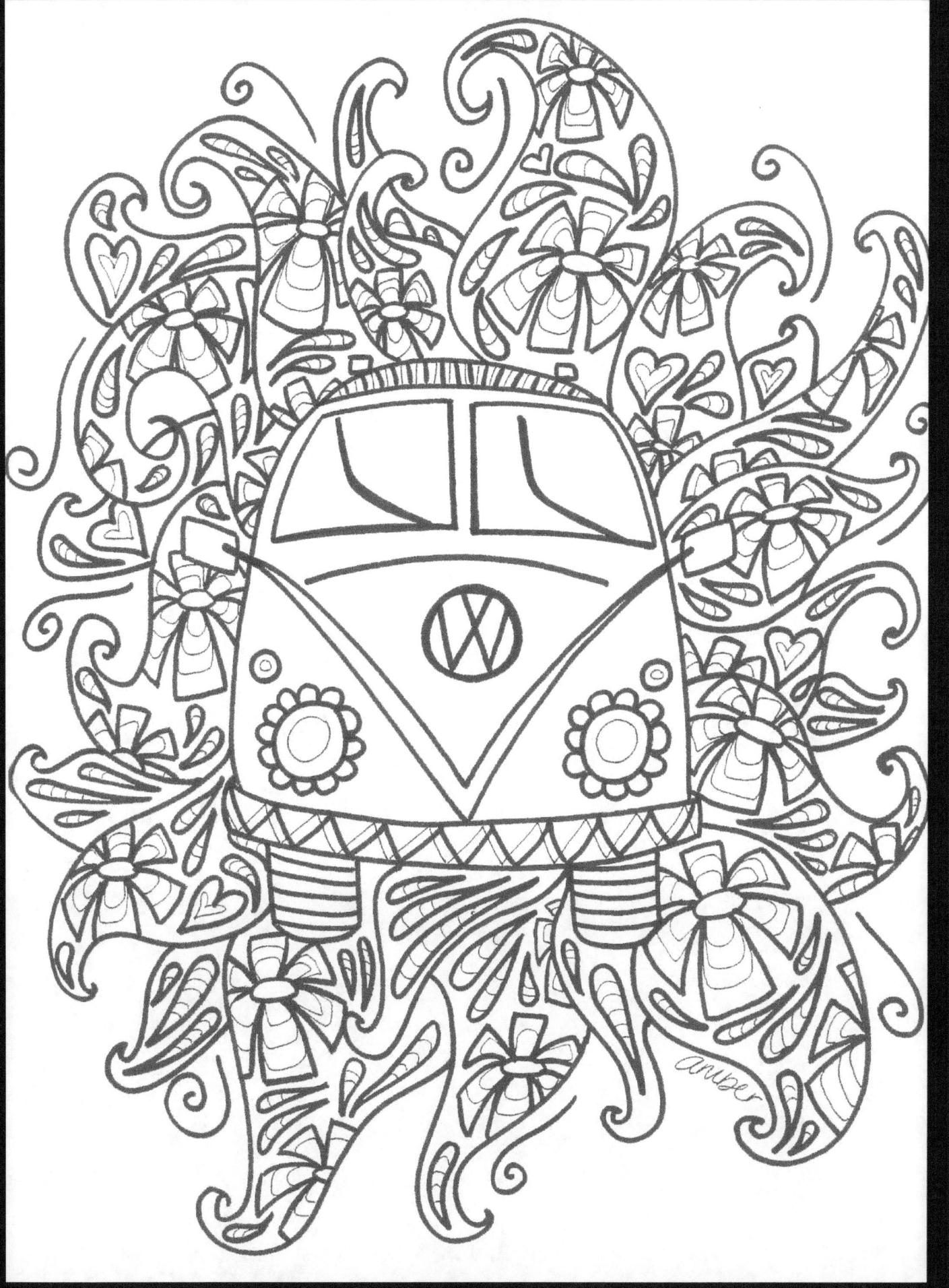

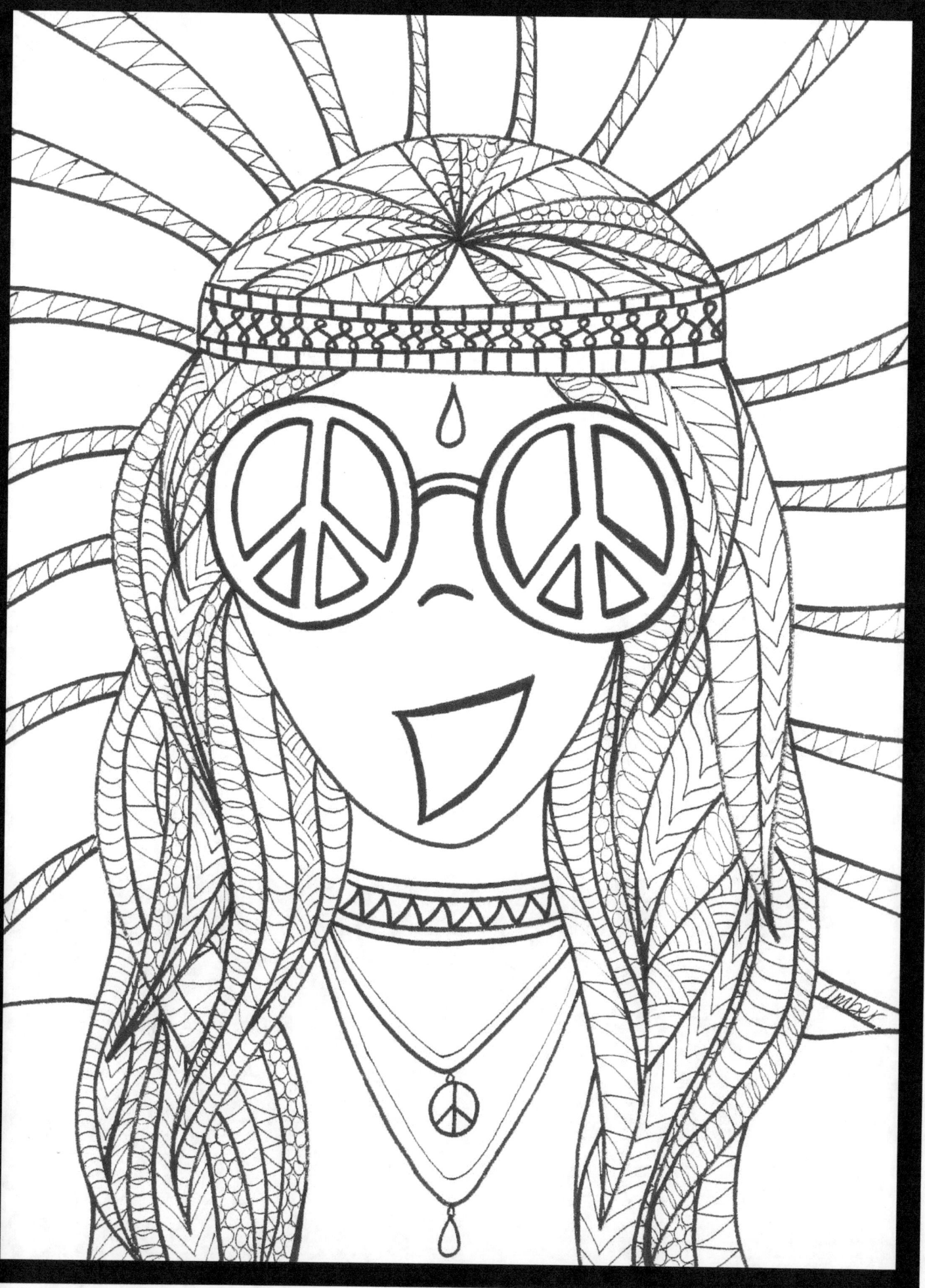

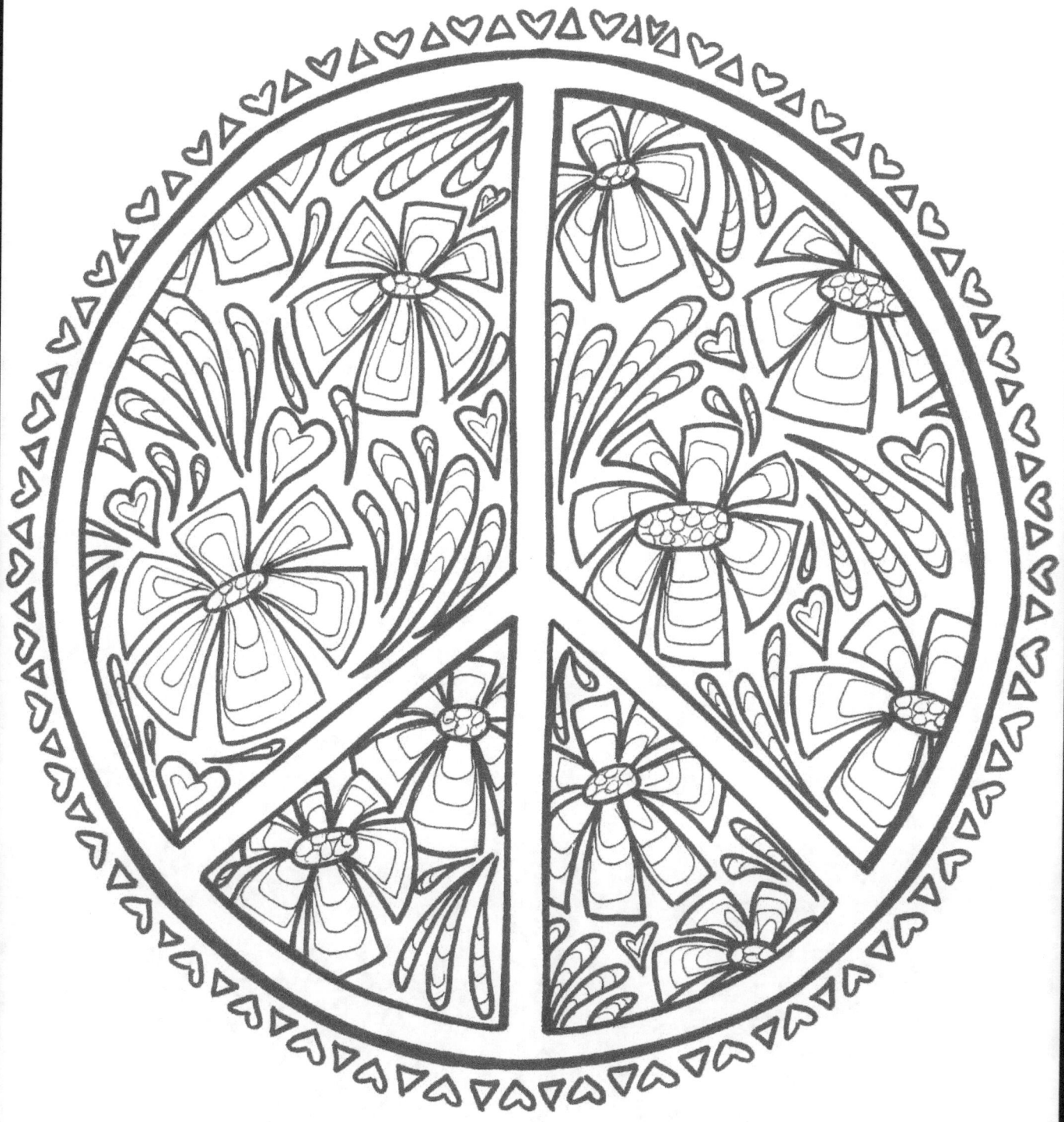

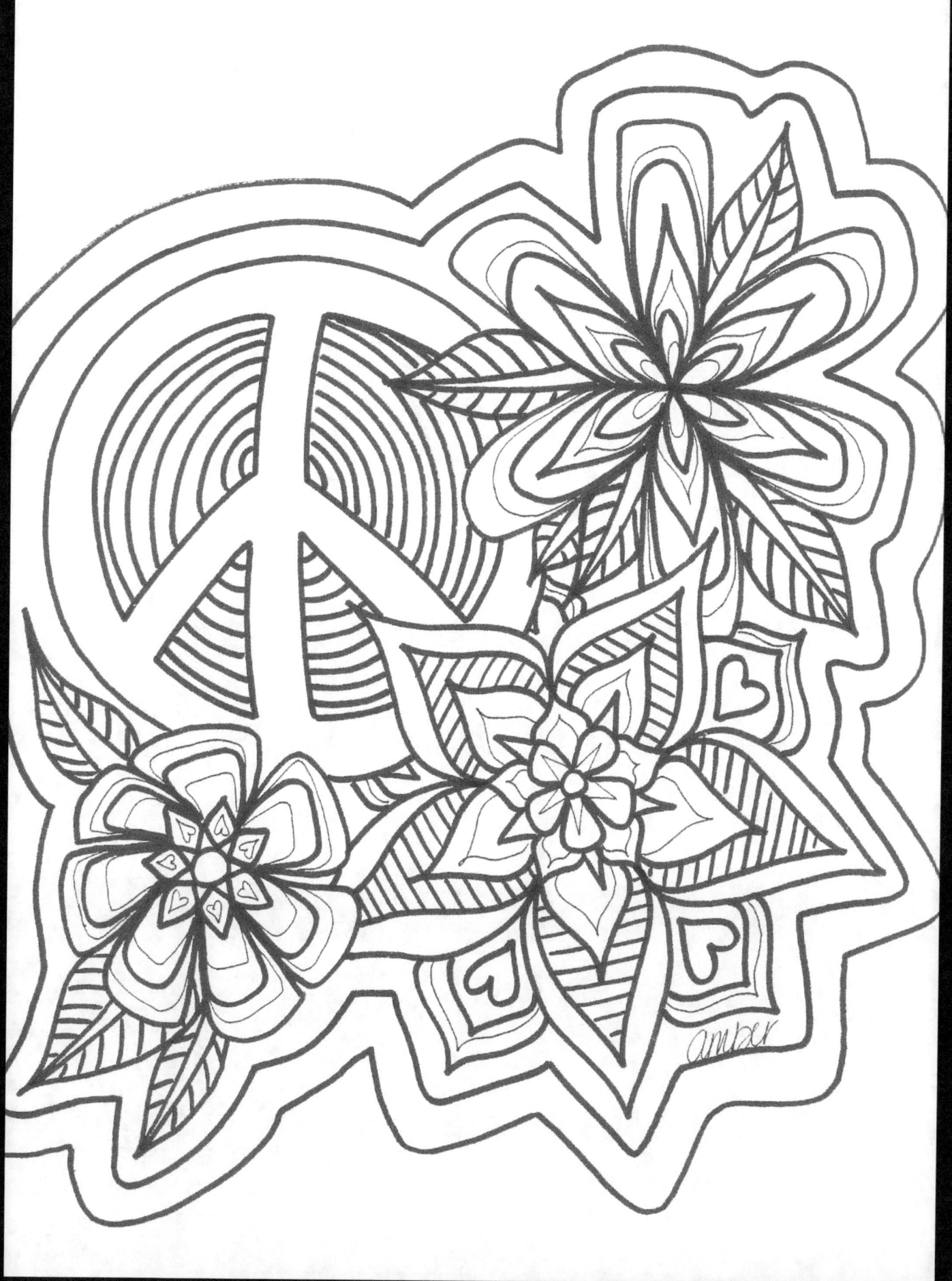

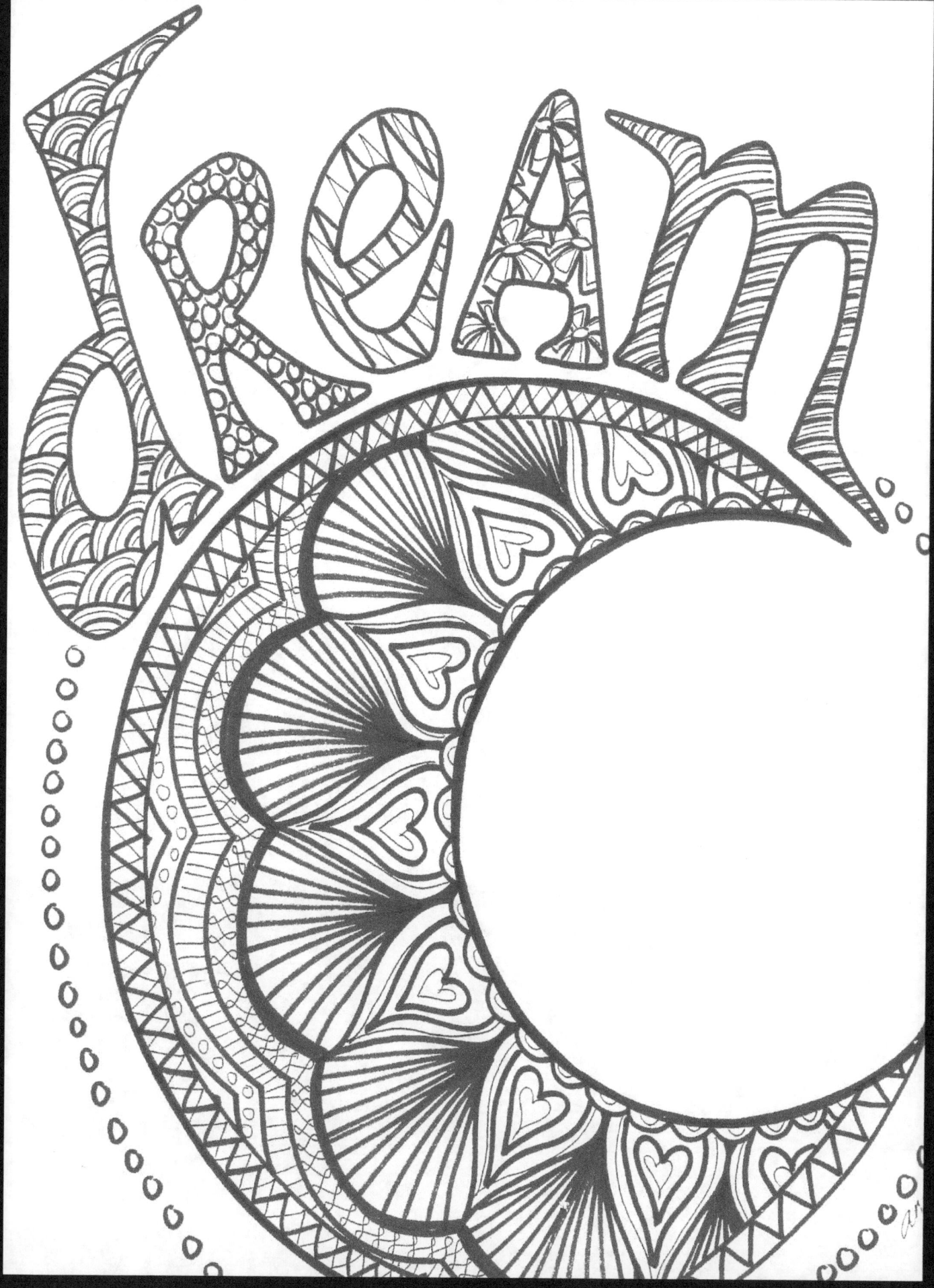

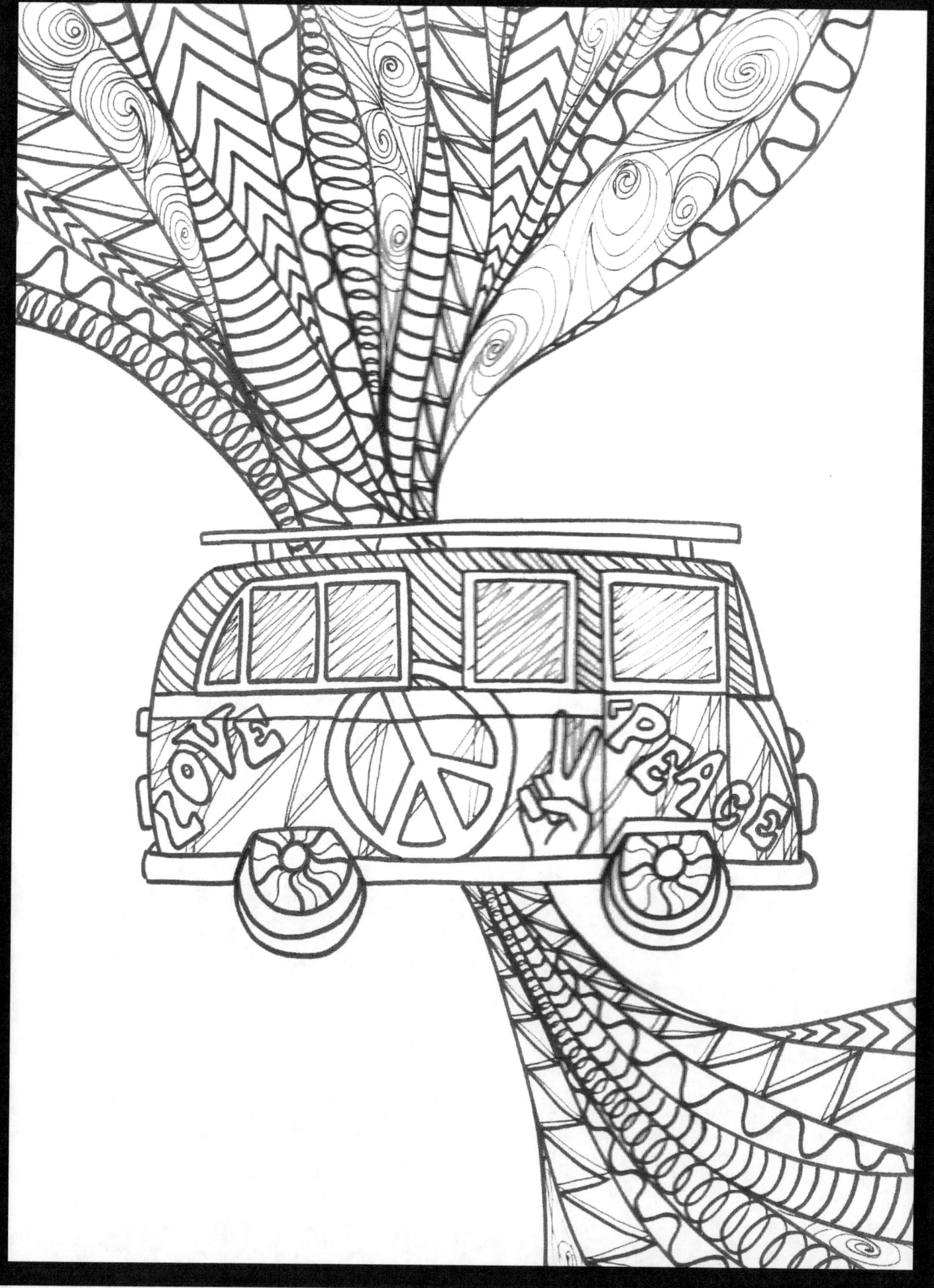

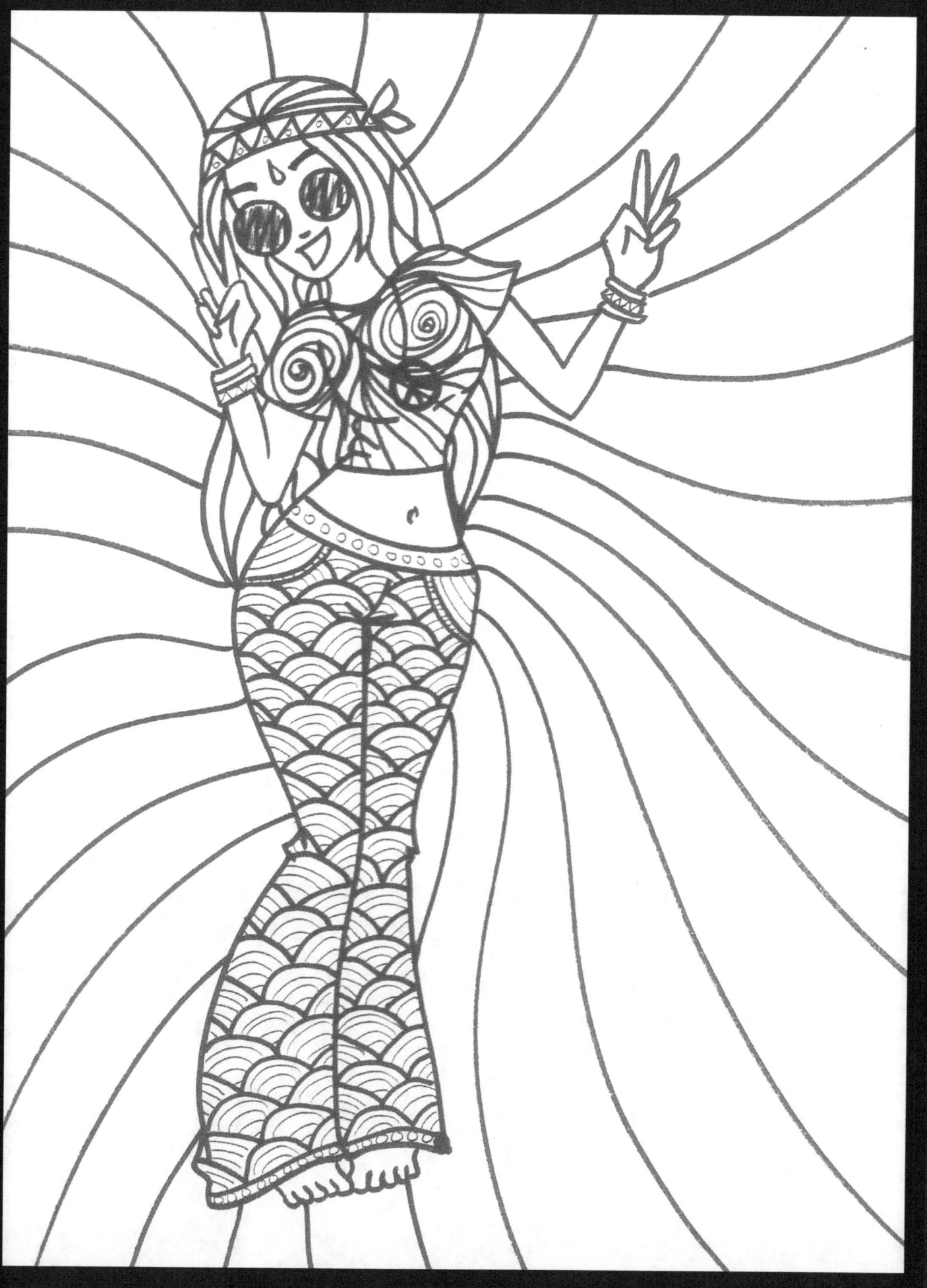

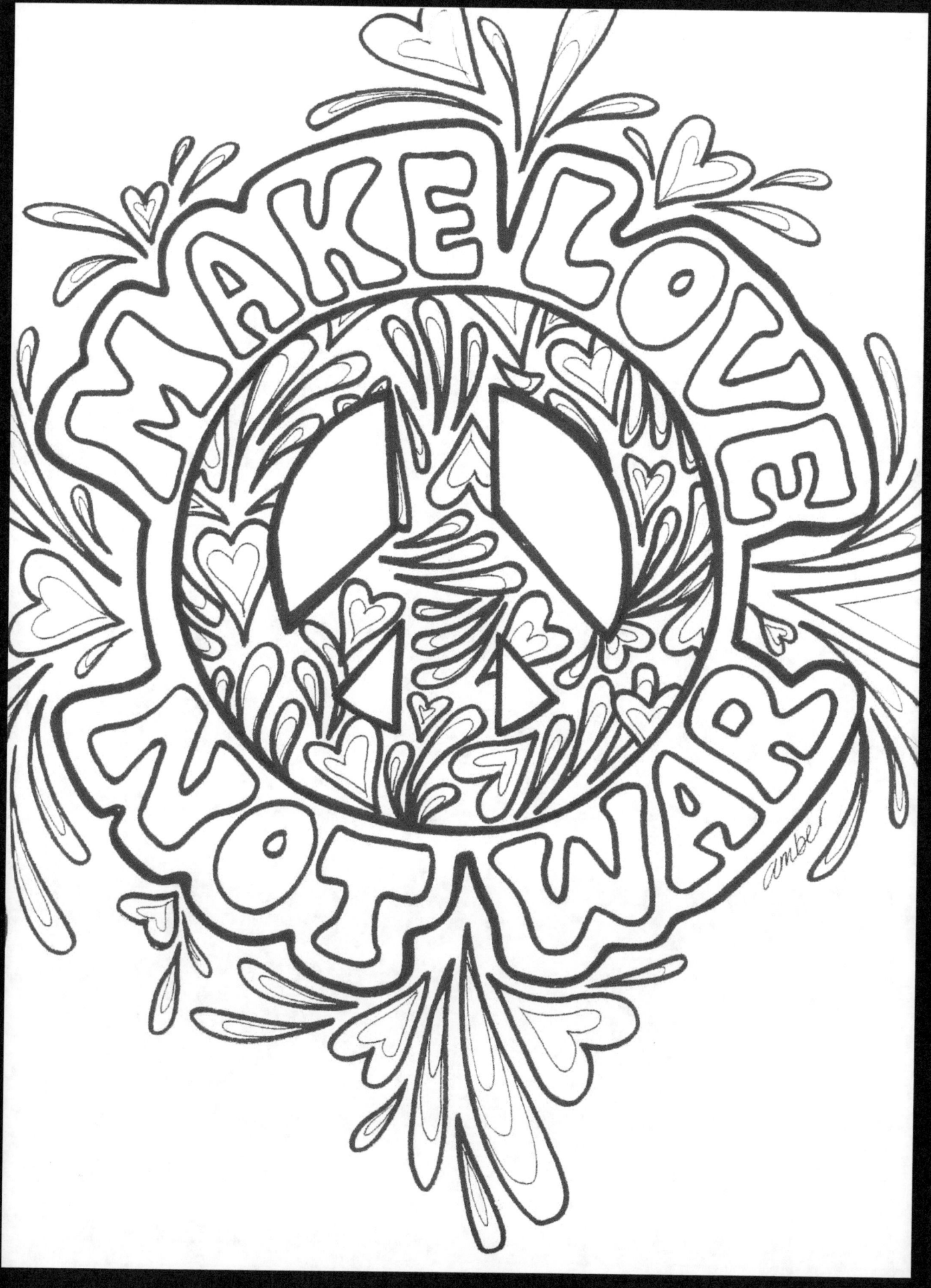

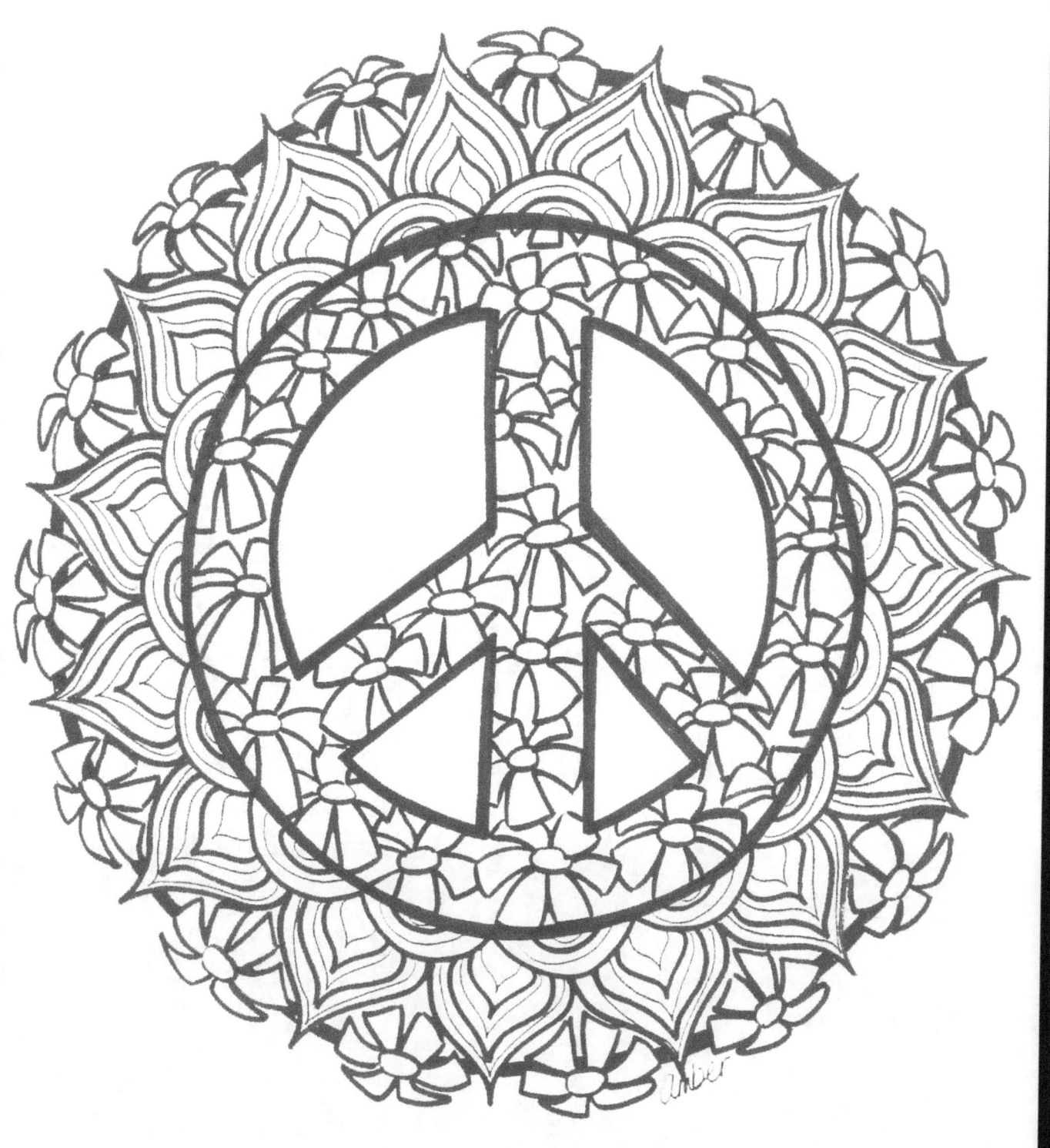

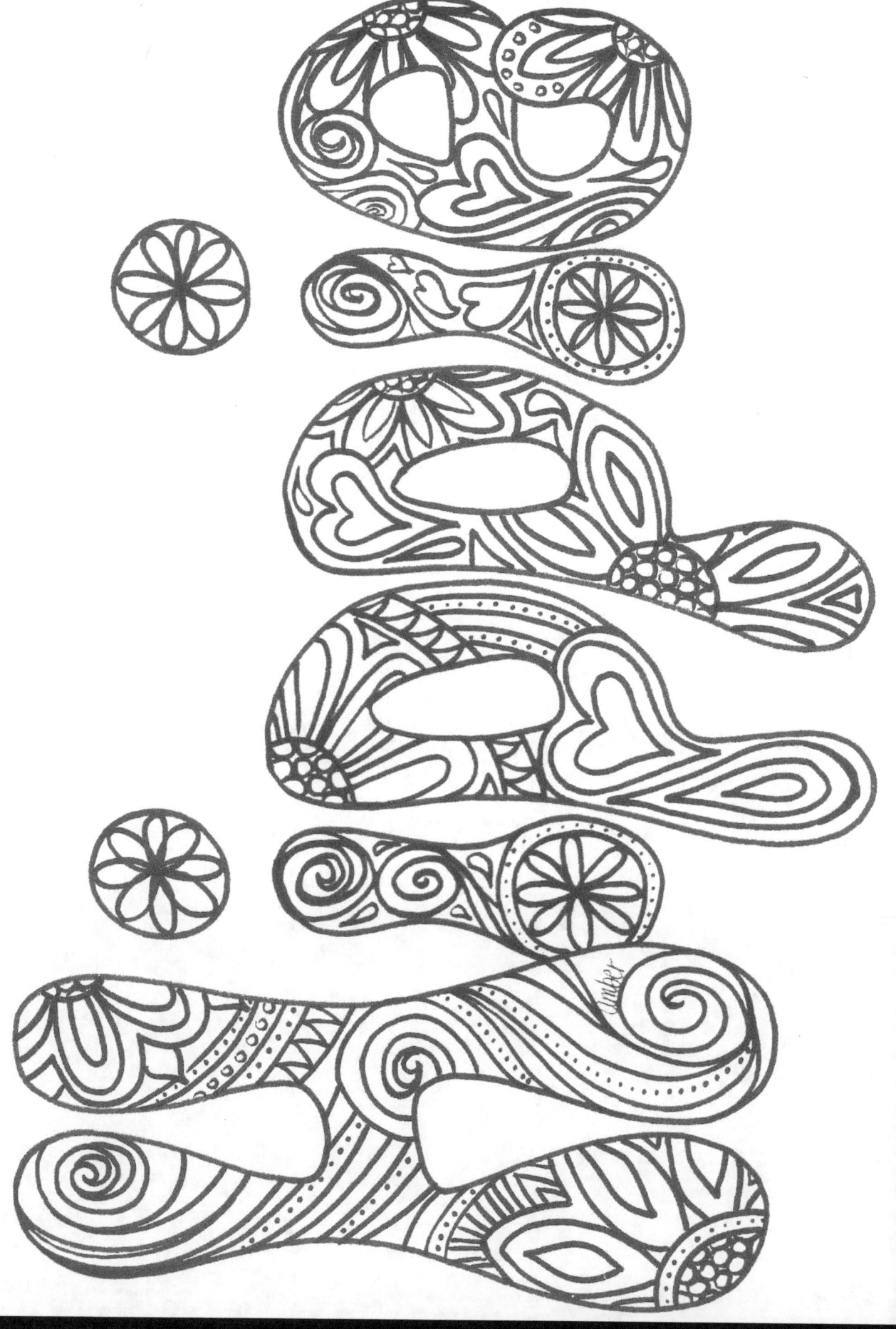

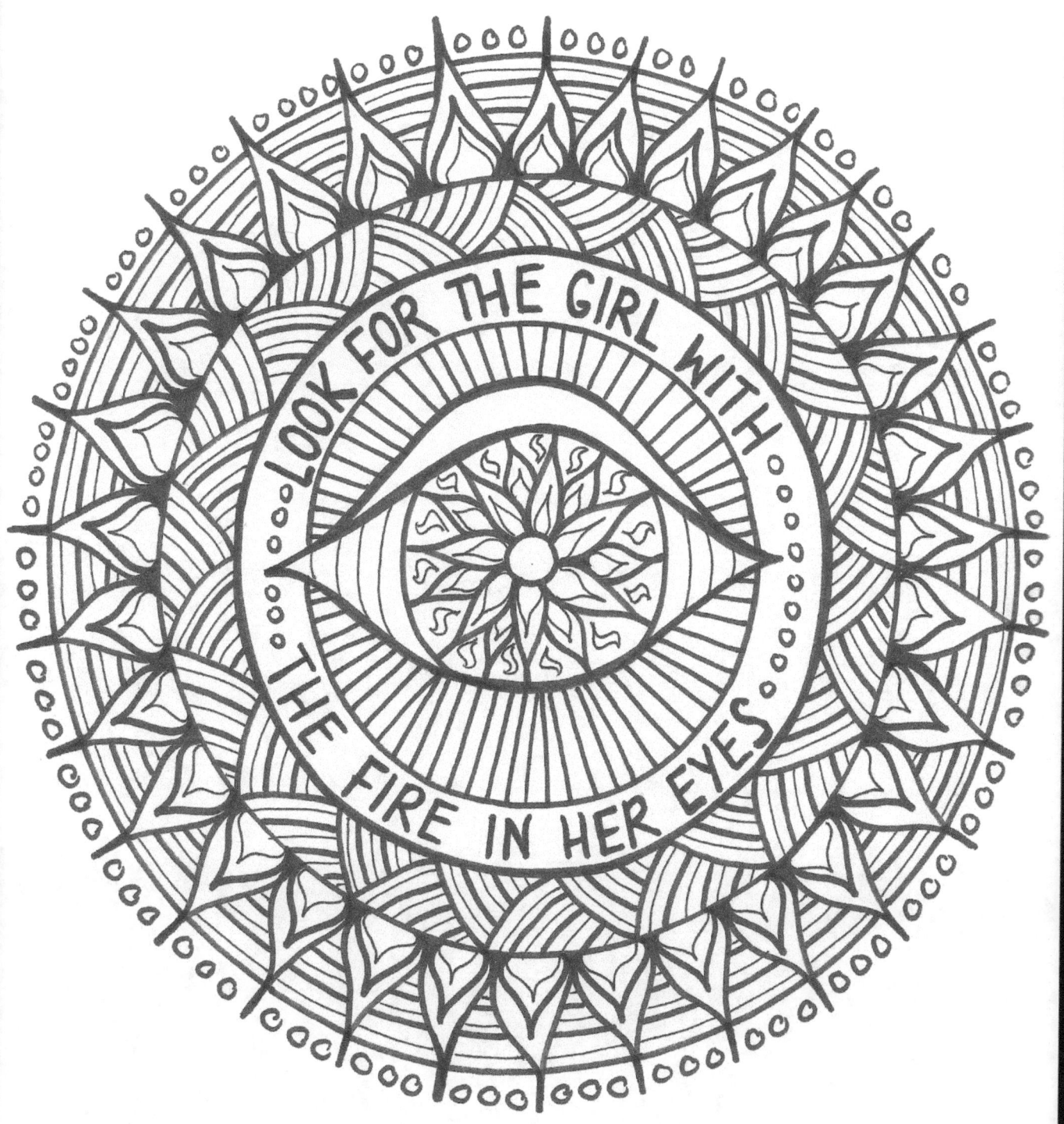

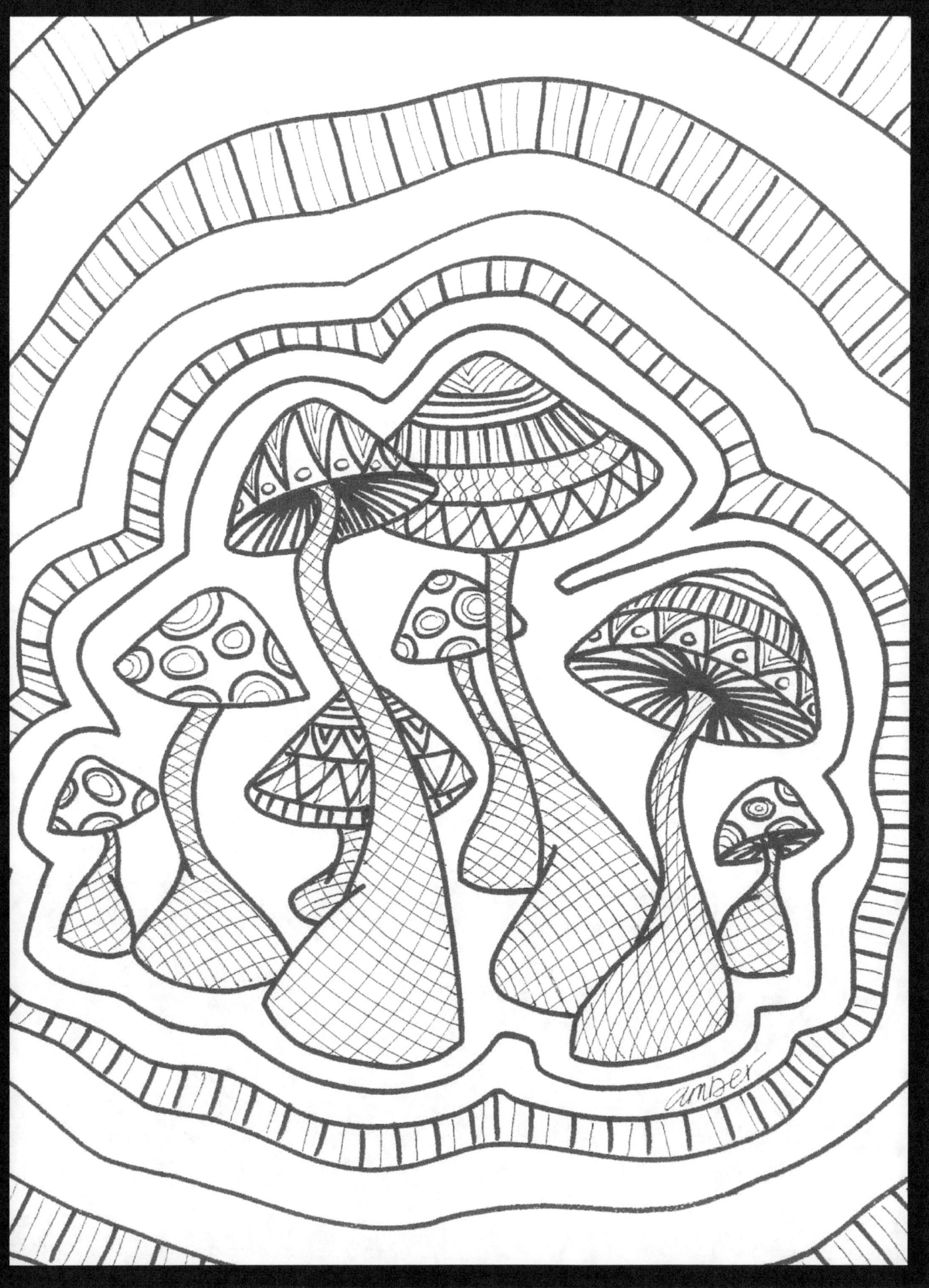

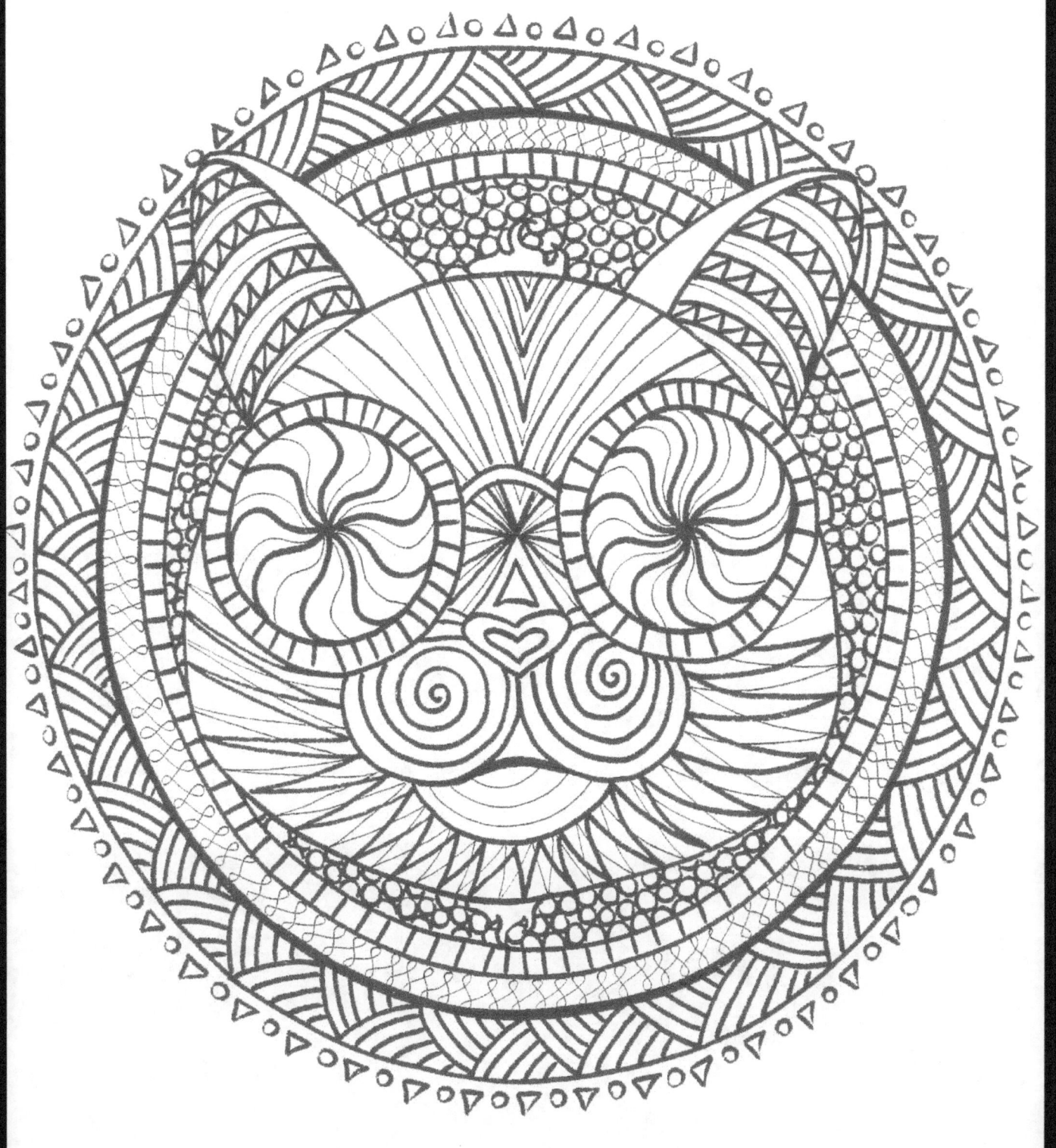